"Looking for a way to combine your favorite drink with dessert? You've found it in this beautifully photographed book. From diner-style favorites to late night concoctions, Kelly has proven that just about any drink can be made into an even better dessert!"

—JONI MARIE NEWMAN, author of *The Complete Guide to Vegan Food Substitutions* and *The Best Veggie Burgers on the Planet*

"Kelly's recipes are accessible and fun, and prove that cuisine without cruelty is the way of the future—and what a delicious future it will be!"

—JASMIN SINGER and MARIANN SULLIVAN, co-founders of Our Hen House

"*Cheers to Vegan Sweets* is boozy perfection. I am *eating* my way through the day with her delicious and innovative recipes—starting with Pumpkin Spice Beercakes and ending with Pina Colada Tres Leches Cake. I can't get enough!"

—LAURA BECK, Vegansaurus.com

"Look, I'm vegan and I've had Kelly's cupcakes, so I can vouch for their staggering awesomeness; but here's the thing—all issues of health and animal welfare aside, this is an incredibly innovative and exciting cookbook filled with recipes that are, dare I say... fun? Seriously, just let this idea wash over you: Chipotle Lime Hot Chocolate Fudge Cookies. Though you may never have enough time to make every recipe in this book, you'll want to try."

—TED LEO, lead singer of Ted Leo and the Pharmacists

CHEERS to VEGAN SWEETS

Drink-Inspired Vegan Desserts

From the Café to the Cocktail Lounge,
Turn Your Sweet Sips into Even
Better Bites!

KELLY PELOZA

FAIR WINDS
PRESS
BEVERLY, MASSACHUSETTS

First published in the USA in 2013 by
Fair Winds Press, a member of
Quayside Publishing Group
100 Cummings Center
Suite 406-L
Beverly, MA 01915-6101
www.fairwindspress.com

17 16 15 14 13   1 2 3 4 5

ISBN: 978-1-59233-568-8

Digital edition published in 2013
eISBN: 978-1-61058-865-2

Library of Congress Cataloging-in-Publication Data
Peloza, Kelly.
  Cheers to vegan sweets! : drink-inspired vegan desserts : from the cafe to the cocktail lounge, turn your sweet sips into
even better bites! / Kelly Peloza.
       pages cm
  Summary: "This innovative vegan baking book features 125 deliciously fun drink-inspired dessert recipes. It's a cookbook
that takes readers on a delicious tour of cafes, cocktail bars, and lemonade stands, where all the drinks come in dessert
form. Imagine your morning vanilla hazelnut mocha re-imagined as a muffin, or relax on the beach with a margarita biscotti,
or stop by the bar and order your brew in Guinness cake form. Instead of sipping your drink, now you can indulge in it!
Author and vegan baker extraordinaire Kelly Peloza has carefully formulated each recipe to deliciously highlight the flavors
of its drink counterpart. From Apple Cider Doughnuts to Chai Spice Baklava to Gingerbread Stout Cake, you'll be amazed
at how deliciously well your sips transform into sweet, satisfied—and vegan!—bites. And with alcoholic- and non-alcoholic
recipes, you're sure to find something perfect for every party and special occasion." —Provided by publisher.
  ISBN 978-1-59233-568-8 (pbk.)
  1. Desserts. 2. Vegan cooking. 3. Baking. I. Title.
  TX773.P425 2013
  641.86--dc23
                        2013024830

Cover design by Debbie Berne Design
Book design by Rita Sowins / Sowins Design
Photography by Kelly Peloza

Printed and bound in China

For my family, friends,
Gnocchi, and Drake

Contents

Introduction

I'D LIKE TO TAKE YOU ON A DELICIOUS TOUR OF TASTE. From cafés to nighttime hotspots, we'll journey to a dream world where all the drinks come in dessert form. Imagine enjoying your morning mocha in a cupcake, or relaxing on the beach with some margarita biscotti, or stopping by the bar and ordering your brew in a brownie. Cake, doughnuts, whoopie pies, mousse, ice cream, bread, and many more drink-inspired desserts are here at your fingertips, and they're all vegan, so everyone can make and enjoy!

I've scoured drink menus at restaurants, cafés, and bars, researched the origins of liquors and mixed drinks, and experimented endlessly to merge some of our most beloved drinks with the delicious textures, flavors, and sensations of vegan baking. So sit back and relax while the photographs and recipes guide you through the dark and moody flavors of chocolate stout, the levity of lemonade, the bells and whistles of a tropical cocktail, and so much more.

Spatulas and cocktail umbrellas at the ready! Double cheers to animal-friendly, decadent desserts!

CHAPTER 1

kitchen basics

When writing the recipes in this book, I strove to strike a balance between ease and creativity, so there's something for everyone, whether you're new to vegan baking or penning your own cookbooks. Here's what you need to know to get started on creating delicious desserts with animal-friendly ingredients so that you can indulge both your taste buds and your ethics.

Essential Ingredients

While many ingredients used in vegan baking probably live in your kitchen already, you'll find some ingredients in this book that are still emerging into culinary familiarity. That said, most can be found in any well-stocked grocery store.

FLOUR

Unbleached all-purpose flour is the dedicated flour in this book. Although the words "dessert" and "healthy" rarely belong in the same sentence, you can get away with replacing some of the white flour in these recipes with whole wheat pastry flour.

Not to be confused with regular whole wheat flour, whole wheat pastry flour is finer, lighter, and doesn't have a strong wheat flavor. Up to half the white flour in a dessert recipe may be replaced with whole wheat pastry flour if you are looking for a healthier alternative. Muffin, pancake, and waffle recipes are equipped to handle a half to a full substitution of whole wheat pastry flour.

> **PRACTICING PORTION CONTROL**
> I have an all-or-nothing approach to dessert: I want decadent dessert or none at all. Rather than compromising flavor and texture by cutting sugar and fat and substituting white flour with whole wheat flour, I use these "unhealthy in excess" ingredients, then eat mindfully by controlling portions, reserving indulgent desserts for special occasions, and eating healthy foods the majority of the time.

SUGAR

When it comes to baking, not all sugars are created equal. Different types of sugar can affect the texture, moisture content, flavor, and level of sweetness in the final product. Some sugars even have a bit of nutritional value (though sweets are usually not the place to look for substantial nutrition!).

Granulated Sugar/Evaporated Cane Juice

The most common form of sugar used in baking, and most often used throughout this book, is granulated white sugar. Some vegans avoid white sugar due to some manufacturers' use of bone char in the processing (although it does not end up in the final product). If this is a concern of yours, beet sugar or organic evaporated cane juice can be used instead.

Brown Sugar

Coated in molasses and endowed with caramel flavor, brown sugar is often used in chewy cookies, caramels, muffins, and spice cakes.

Turbinado or "Raw" Sugar

I like coarse turbinado sugar for sprinkling atop muffins, cookies, and quick breads, as it adds a sweet crunch to mild-flavored baked goods and breakfast items. I wouldn't recommend using it in place of granulated sugar in baked goods, however, as it won't really dissolve, adding an undesirable graininess to cakes and cookies.

Agave Nectar

Increasingly available in mainstream grocery stores, agave nectar is the closest vegan substitute for honey. It adds a delicate flavor and quite a bit of moisture to baked goods.

Maple Syrup

By far the most expensive sweetener, maple syrup has many uses in the kitchen beyond accompanying pancakes and waffles. It makes a great sugar substitute in pumpkin or apple desserts, muffins and other breakfast and brunch items, and any other baked goods that would benefit from a hint of maple flavor.

Corn Syrup or Brown Rice Syrup

Corn syrup is widely out of favor due to its unhealthy attributes, so I use it sparingly, saving it for candy making and special desserts, like Fried Coca-Cola (page 96), where health concerns are already out the window. Brown rice syrup has a similar consistency and makes a more nutritionally sound substitution for corn syrup.

FATS

With the vegan demographic growing, food manufacturers are offering a variety of vegan-friendly oils, margarines, and fats. Following are some of the choices that I prefer.

Non-hydrogenated Margarine

I use Earth Balance brand margarine exclusively, as the flavor and texture mimic butter in baking much better than anything I've tried. While not an everyday item due to the cost and fat content, it's made of non-hydrogenated, non-GMO (genetically modified organism) oils, so it's a good, clean choice when baking.

Non-hydrogenated Shortening

Typically used to create stability in buttercream frostings or make piecrusts flaky, vegan shortening is possible to find without turning to hydrogenated oils (aka trans fats). Spectrum and Earth Balance offer non-hydrogenated shortenings.

Neutral-flavored Oil

Canola oil is my personal favorite vegetable oil to use in baking, sometimes taking the place of butter or margarine. GMOs are sometimes a concern with canola oil, but that can be avoided by seeking out organic versions. Safflower, sunflower, and peanut oils are also neutral, but not as common.

SUBSTITUTING AND REPLACING FATS

Vegan margarine isn't available in all areas, and it can become expensive, especially if you bake often. The good news is that neutral oils can often replace margarine in baked good recipes without compromising results. The substitution works best in cakes and cookies. Replace the margarine (or other solid fat) in a recipe with two-thirds the amount of oil. For example, if a recipe calls for 1 cup (225 g) margarine, use ⅔ cup (160 ml) canola oil.

If you're looking to make your baked goods low-fat, you can replace oil or margarine in a recipe with the same amount of applesauce or vegan yogurt. Be aware, however, that this will make the product much cakier. For best results, start by replacing half the fat with applesauce or yogurt. For example, if a recipe calls for ½ cup (120 ml) canola oil, use ¼ cup (60 ml) canola oil and ¼ cup (61 g) applesauce.

Coconut Oil

Solid at room temperature, coconut oil has properties somewhere between canola oil and margarine and adds a strong, sweet coconut flavor. It works beautifully in piecrusts, shortbread, and anything crispy and flaky.

NONDAIRY MILK

Almond, soy, rice, hemp, oat, coconut, hazelnut, or any other nondairy milk you can think of can be used interchangeably in these recipes. With several different options emerging in supermarkets, soy is no longer the default vegan milk.

In some recipes, I specify which milk to use, but it's really just a recommendation. My personal favorite is almond, but I use soy when baking for people with nut allergies.

FRESH FRUIT

Although this is a dessert book, incorporating fresh produce and wholesome ingredients into sweets makes a huge difference in taste and breaks the monotony of chocolate and buttercream.

SPICES

I highly encourage purchasing spices (whole and/or ground) in bulk and shopping at spice stores. The quality is greater than the tiny prepackaged jars you'll find in the baking aisle of the grocery store. For instance, I strongly disliked ground nutmeg until I started grating my own whole nutmeg fresh. Bulk buying is also far cheaper—I've found great deals on bulk spices at Mexican, Indian, and Italian markets.

NUTS

Peanut butter, hazelnuts, almonds, amaretto, and almond extract show up a few times in this recipe collection, but not often. If you or anyone you know has nut allergies, you picked up the right baking book! Quite simply, drinks rarely contain nuts, so recipes based on drinks are frequently nut-free.

Equipment

A pleasing fact for the devoted minimalist is that most vegan baking can be done with basic kitchen tools, such as a mixing bowl, spoon, and baking pans. If you want to go beyond the basics, there are several culinary apparatuses that make daunting kitchen tasks a breeze and pamper the dedicated baker. I'll share a few of my favorite staples as well as some nifty devices here.

UTENSILS

Mixing spoons, spatulas, and sharp knives are the most basic kitchen tools, but absolutely necessary for baking.

BAKING PANS

For the variety of recipes in this book, you'll need cookie sheets, cupcake pans (and liners), 8-inch (20.5 cm) round cake pans, an 8 x 4-inch (20.5 x 10 cm) loaf pan, and an 8-inch (20.5 cm) square pan. I'd even argue the necessity of 6-inch (15 cm) mini round cake pans, as I use them more than the standard size, but understand that most people probably don't.

STAND MIXER

Although not absolutely necessary, a stand mixer is a great tool to evenly mix your batters, knead dough, and whip frosting. The alternatives are handheld beaters or a good old mixing bowl and spoon.

FOOD PROCESSOR

A food processor is great for making cookie crumbs, puréeing vegetables and fruits, making hummus, and a variety of other kitchen tasks. They can be difficult to clean, but sometimes nothing else will do.

PARCHMENT PAPER OR SILICONE BAKING MAT

Lining cookie sheets and cake pans with parchment paper will prevent the finished product from sticking to the pan. It makes cookie bottoms perfectly golden brown, and sheets can be reused a few times. You could use a silicone baking mat in place of parchment, if you'd like. I use silicone mats for chocolate and candy making and as a workspace for sculpting fondant, but I prefer parchment for baking.

MICROPLANE GRATER

When you're zesting citrus, grating ginger, or incorporating fresh nutmeg into your baked goods, a Microplane grater is an invaluable tool. It effortlessly grates and zests, and you'll laugh at all those years you used a dull cheese grater to zest lemons (unless that was just me).

COOKIE AND ICE CREAM SCOOPS

A small (1 tablespoon, or 15 ml) mechanical-release cookie scoop is great to have for perfectly portioned cookie dough. Use a large scoop (¼ cup, or 60 ml) or ice cream scoop to fill cupcake liners for the perfect amount of batter and little mess.

Kitchen Tips and Troubleshooting

Baking is truly an art, and recipes are dependent on precise formulas and science. While there are many variables you can change within a recipe, don't mess with science! Just as an arch will collapse without the keystone, a cake will not rise with a drastically altered ratio of wet to dry ingredients, or without a leavening agent, so substitute with care. Following are few additional tips for baking success.

CHECK YOUR LEAVENING AGENTS

The two most common ingredients used to leaven baked goods are baking soda and baking powder. Baking soda reacts with an acid to create bubbles of leavening gas, and (double-acting) baking powder reacts with water, then again with the heat of the oven.

If your baking powder or soda has been in your pantry for longer than you can remember, you can test drive them to see if they're active. Pour some vinegar and baking soda together in a small bowl and see if it bubbles. If it does, congratulations, you've made a volcano (and your baking soda is active)! Baking powder should have the same result with water.

USE AN OVEN THERMOMETER

Even if you set your oven to 350°F (180°C), it may not necessarily maintain that temperature. Ovens vary by manufacturer and age, so check if your oven is accurate by keeping an oven thermometer inside. Adjust any temperature discrepancies for best results.

BEWARE OF OVER-MIXING

When you agitate (stir or knead) a dough containing wheat flour, it activates the gluten in the flour. If the dough is overly agitated, it becomes sticky and dense. This reaction is exactly what you want when making bread, but it will lend a gummy texture to cookies and cakes. Over-mixing is a mistake beginners make often, stirring excessively to make sure the batter is just right, but it is preferable to leave some lumps in the batter than to over-mix. Make a habit of stirring your ingredients until they're just barely combined.

Happy Baking!

Equipped with a stocked pantry and all the tools of the trade, you're ready to create a world of drink-inspired delight! Enjoy creating a sweet and substantial afternoon snack, or a complex dessert to finish a fancy meal. With chocolate, fresh fruit, and zesty sweets, impress everyone around you with decadent desserts that they better believe are vegan!

CHAPTER 2

the breakfast bar

Brunch favorites are paired with brunch drinks in delightful mid-morning treats. Biscuits, muffins, doughnuts, pancakes, and waffles grace the table with unique flavors.

Strawberry Banana Smoothie Waffles

A waffle iron is a great investment. Once you get the hang of making waffles, it's easy to make huge batches at a time, and they beat the boxed version any day. This recipe captures the flavors of strawberry banana smoothies.

YIELD: 8 TO 12 WAFFLES

2 CUPS (250 G) FLOUR

½ CUP (70 G) CORNMEAL

½ CUP (40 G) WHOLE OR QUICK-COOKING OATS

1 TABLESPOON (14 G) BAKING POWDER

¼ TEASPOON BAKING SODA

¼ TEASPOON CINNAMON

¼ TEASPOON SALT

1 TABLESPOON (15 ML) LEMON JUICE

1½ CUPS (355 ML) NONDAIRY MILK

2 RIPE BANANAS

1 CUP (43 G) SLICED STRAWBERRIES, DIVIDED

2 TABLESPOONS (30 ML) CANOLA OIL

½ TEASPOON LEMON ZEST

OIL OR NONSTICK SPRAY, FOR GREASING

Combine the flour, cornmeal, oats, baking powder, baking soda, cinnamon, and salt in a large mixing bowl and whisk together. Set aside.

Pour the lemon juice into the milk and let sit for 5 minutes to curdle. In a separate bowl, mash the bananas and ¼ cup (11 g) of the sliced strawberries together.

Create a well in the center of the dry ingredients and pour in the curdled milk, mashed banana, the ¼ cup (11 g) strawberries, oil, and zest. Whisk together the wet and dry ingredients, incorporating the remaining ¾ cup (32 g) sliced strawberries as you go. The batter should be thick.

Preheat your waffle iron, brush or spray with oil, and cook according to the manufacturer's instructions. Top with maple or fruit syrup, sliced bananas and strawberries, and a sprinkle of grated lemon zest.

Pumpkin Spice Beercakes

Make these pancakes in autumn, when pumpkin beer is widely available. The flavors and spices of pumpkin pie translate wonderfully to a savory but slightly sweet pancake.

YIELD: 12 TO 15 PANCAKES

1½ CUPS (187.5 G) FLOUR

½ CUP (62.5 G) WHOLE WHEAT PASTRY FLOUR (OR MORE WHITE FLOUR)

1 TABLESPOON (14 G) BAKING POWDER

1 TABLESPOON (9 G) CORNMEAL

2 TABLESPOONS (30 G) BROWN SUGAR

2 TEASPOONS CINNAMON

½ TEASPOON GINGER

¼ TEASPOON FRESHLY GRATED NUTMEG

⅛ TEASPOON CLOVES

¼ TEASPOON SALT

¾ CUP (184 G) PUMPKIN PURÉE

1 TABLESPOON (15 ML) AGAVE NECTAR

1 TEASPOON VANILLA EXTRACT

1 CUP (235 ML) NONDAIRY MILK

⅔ CUP (160 ML) PUMPKIN BEER

¼ TEASPOON LEMON ZEST

1 TABLESPOON (14 G) VEGAN MARGARINE

MAPLE SYRUP (OPTIONAL)

CHOPPED APPLES (OPTIONAL)

VEGAN WHIPPED CREAM (OPTIONAL)

CINNAMON (OPTIONAL)

Combine the flours, baking powder, cornmeal, brown sugar, spices, and salt in a large mixing bowl. Stir together with a whisk.

Make a well in the middle of the dry ingredients and add the pumpkin, agave nectar, vanilla, milk, beer, and lemon zest. Mix wet and dry ingredients until just combined.

Preheat an electric griddle or two medium skillets over medium heat. Rub some margarine on one of the pans and melt the rest in the other. Pour melted vegan margarine into the pancake batter and stir until combined.

Pour about ¼ cup (60 ml) batter (or any amount you'd like) per pancake onto each pan. Flip when bubbles start to form and the pancakes hold their shape. Repeat with the remaining batter. Keep warm on a plate in the oven set to its lowest temperature while you make the rest of the pancakes.

Serve with autumnal toppings, such as maple syrup, chopped apples, whipped cream, and cinnamon.

REPLACING THE ALCOHOL
Use ⅔ cup (160 ml) nondairy milk instead of pumpkin beer.

RECIPE NOTES
- If pumpkin beer is out of season, or you can't find it near you, regular beer is a fine substitution.
- All pancake batters cook a bit differently, so feel free to check the underside of your pancakes while they cook so you can brown them to your liking.

Coconut Chocolate Stout Pancakes

Coconut is a natural complement to the rich flavor of chocolate stout, and even better wrapped up in a sweet breakfast treat. You can use either canned or carton coconut milk in these pancakes; the former will make them slightly richer, but will also add extra fat.

YIELD: 10 TO 12 PANCAKES

1⅔ CUPS (208 G) FLOUR

⅓ CUP (39 G) COCOA POWDER

1 TABLESPOON (14 G) BAKING POWDER

1 TABLESPOON (9 G) CORNMEAL

¼ TEASPOON SALT

3 TABLESPOONS (45 ML) AGAVE NECTAR

⅓ CUP (77 G) NONDAIRY YOGURT

1 TEASPOON VANILLA EXTRACT

¾ TEASPOON COCONUT EXTRACT

1 CUP (235 ML) CHOCOLATE STOUT

⅔ CUP (160 ML) COCONUT MILK

1 TABLESPOON (14 G) COCONUT BUTTER, COCONUT OIL, OR VEGAN MARGARINE

MAPLE SYRUP (OPTIONAL)

SHREDDED COCONUT (OPTIONAL)

NUTS (OPTIONAL)

CHOCOLATE SYRUP (OPTIONAL)

Combine flour, cocoa powder, baking powder, cornmeal, and salt, stirring with a whisk. Make a well in the middle and add the agave nectar, yogurt, extracts, stout, and coconut milk. Stir until almost combined.

Preheat an electric griddle or two medium skillets over medium heat. Rub some coconut butter on one of the pans and melt the rest in the other. Pour melted coconut butter into the pancake batter and stir until combined.

Pour ¼ cup (60 ml) batter per pancake onto each pan and flip when bubbles start to form on top, 3 to 5 minutes per side, depending on the size of your pancakes. Keep warm on a plate in the oven, set to its lowest temperature, while you make the rest of the pancakes.

Spread a bit of coconut butter on the pancakes, then top with pure maple syrup, shredded coconut, nuts, and chocolate syrup.

RECIPE NOTE
If you can't find chocolate stout, regular stout is a fine substitution. Just add an additional tablespoon of cocoa powder.

REPLACING THE ALCOHOL
Substitute nondairy chocolate milk for the stout.

Spiced Rum and Sweet Potato Pie French Toast

Sweet potato, maple syrup, fresh spices, and a coconut cream topping infuse the essence of autumn into this scrumptious brunch dish. It's an absolute treat when made with thick sourdough or seedy, crusty bread. Serve with coffee, hot apple cider, or mimosas made with pumpkin beer.

YIELD: 12 TO 14 SLICES

1 BATCH COCONUT WHIPPED CREAM
   (PAGE 167), CHILLED
1½ CUPS (337.5 G) COOKED, MASHED
   SWEET POTATO (1 LARGE OR
   2 MEDIUM)
⅓ CUP (80 ML) SPICED RUM
⅓ CUP (80 ML) MAPLE SYRUP
½ CUP (120 ML) SOY OR COCONUT
   CREAMER
½ CUP (120 ML) NONDAIRY MILK
¼ CUP (60 ML) APPLE CIDER
2 TABLESPOONS (15.5 G) FLOUR
1 TEASPOON CINNAMON
3 TABLESPOONS (42 G) VEGAN
   MARGARINE, COCONUT OIL, OR
   COCONUT SPREAD
2 TEASPOONS FRESHLY GRATED GINGER
FRESHLY GRATED NUTMEG, TO TASTE
12 TO 14 SLICES SLIGHTLY STALE BREAD
VEGAN MARGARINE, FOR COOKING
MAPLE SYRUP (OPTIONAL)
COCONUT CREAM (OPTIONAL)

Combine all the ingredients except the bread in a blender or food processor and blend until smooth. Adjust the sweetness or spices to your liking. The batter should have the consistency of a thick milk shake.

Pour the batter into a shallow container and soak 3 or 4 slices of bread for about 10 minutes, flipping halfway through. You can soak the next round while the first batch is cooking.

Melt some margarine in a skillet set over medium-low heat. Lift the soaked bread slices out of the batter, letting the excess batter drip off, then place in the pan and cook for 5 to 6 minutes. Flip and cook for an additional 5 minutes on the other side. It's important that the heat is on low so the insides have a chance to cook through.

Place cooked French toast on a serving dish and repeat the process with the remaining slices (or make to order).

Top the French toast with pure maple syrup and a dollop of coconut cream, then serve!

REPLACING THE ALCOHOL
Replace the rum with nondairy milk and add ¼ teaspoon (1 ml) rum extract.

Peanut Butter Banana Smoothie Muffins

This is a muffin version of the famous smoothie and milkshake combination: peanut butter, chocolate, and banana. These muffins are fluffy, flavored with lots of banana and peanut butter, and studded with melty chocolate chips. Purposely overfill the muffin cups for huge muffin tops.

YIELD: 12 MUFFINS

⅔ CUP (173.5 G) PEANUT BUTTER

3 TABLESPOONS (45 ML) OIL

1 CUP (225 G) MASHED BANANAS
   (2 MEDIUM BANANAS)

½ CUP (100 G) SUGAR

⅓ CUP (75 G) BROWN SUGAR

1½ CUPS (355 ML) NONDAIRY MILK

1½ TEASPOONS VANILLA

2⅓ CUPS (292 G) FLOUR

2½ TEASPOONS BAKING POWDER

¾ TEASPOON BAKING SODA

½ TEASPOON SALT

½ CUP (87.5 G) VEGAN CHOCOLATE CHIPS

TURBINADO SUGAR, FOR SPRINKLING
   (OPTIONAL)

Preheat oven to 375°F (190°C, or gas mark 4). Line a muffin pan with cupcake liners and set aside. In a large bowl, stir together the peanut butter, oil, mashed bananas, sugar, brown sugar, milk, and vanilla.

Sift in the flour, baking powder, baking soda, and salt until just combined. The batter should be thick and light brown in color. Stir in the chocolate chips.

Spoon the muffin batter into the liners, filling just over the top of the paper. Sprinkle the tops with turbinado sugar if desired for a little crunch.

Bake for 22 minutes, or until the centers are tall and firm and a toothpick inserted in the center comes out clean.

Hazelnut, Black Tea, and Pear Muffins

Sweet pears and hazelnuts complement the earthy flavor of black tea in these muffins, which are not nearly as strange as they sound.

YIELD: 12 MUFFINS

1 CUP (135 G) HAZELNUTS, CHOPPED

1 CUP (235 ML) HAZELNUT OR OTHER NONDAIRY MILK

2 BLACK TEA BAGS (1 FOR STEEPING, 1 FOR INCORPORATING INTO THE DRY INGREDIENTS)

3 CUPS (375 G) FLOUR

½ CUP (100 G) SUGAR

1 TABLESPOON (14 G) BAKING POWDER

¾ TEASPOON BAKING SODA

¼ TEASPOON CINNAMON

¼ TEASPOON SALT

1 TEASPOON APPLE CIDER VINEGAR

¾ CUP (180 ML) NONDAIRY MILK

3 TABLESPOONS (45 ML) MAPLE SYRUP

⅔ CUP (160 ML) CANOLA OIL

½ TEASPOON LEMON ZEST

2 TEASPOONS VANILLA EXTRACT

1 PEAR, CHOPPED

Preheat oven to 375°F (190°C, or gas mark 5).

Spread the hazelnuts on a baking sheet and toast until fragrant, 8 to 10 minutes. Once cool enough to handle, rub the skins off with a hand towel or paper towel. Chop the hazelnuts finely, leaving a few chunky pieces. Reserve ¼ cup (29 g) chopped hazelnuts for garnish.

Heat 1 cup (235 ml) milk and steep the black tea bag for 5 minutes. Set aside to cool.

Combine the flour, sugar, baking powder, baking soda, cinnamon, contents of the unused black tea bag, and salt in a large mixing bowl. Combine the apple cider vinegar with ¾ cup (180 ml) non-dairy milk and let sit for a couple of minutes, until it begins to curdle.

Make a well in the center of the dry ingredients and pour the vinegar-milk mixture in the well. Add the steeped milk (discarding the tea bag), maple syrup, canola oil, lemon zest, and vanilla. Stir everything together until just combined. Add the chopped pear and ¾ cup (87 g) chopped toasted hazelnuts.

Fill each muffin cup to the top, then sprinkle the remaining hazelnuts evenly over the muffins. Bake for 15 to 18 minutes, let cool for 5 minutes in the pan, then transfer to a wire rack to cool completely.

RECIPE NOTE
For extra hazelnut flavor, add ½ teaspoon hazelnut extract and/or replace 2 tablespoons (30 ml) of the maple syrup with hazelnut syrup.

Bourbon Banana Bread

This recipe was contributed by my dad. Basic banana bread is elevated with the fun and fresh additions of lime and bourbon.

YIELD: 1 LOAF

½ CUP (112 G) VEGAN MARGARINE

1 CUP (200 G) SUGAR

1½ CUPS (338 G) MASHED BANANAS

¼ CUP (60 ML) BOURBON

1 TEASPOON LIME JUICE

2 CUPS (250 G) FLOUR, SIFTED

1 TABLESPOON (13.8 G) BAKING POWDER

½ TEASPOON SALT

1 CUP (120 G) CHOPPED PECANS OR
    WALNUTS

Preheat oven to 375°F (190°C, or gas mark 5). Grease an 8 x 4-inch (20.5 x 10 cm) loaf pan and set aside.

Cream vegan margarine and sugar together. Add mashed bananas, bourbon, and lime juice and blend until smooth.

Sift flour, baking powder, and salt together and mix into banana mixture. Add nuts.

Bake in the greased loaf pan for about 1 hour. Because baking times vary with the moisture of the batter, check the loaf at 45 minutes with a toothpick. If it comes out clean, the bread is ready. If not, continue baking.

RECIPE NOTE
For a variation, replace the bourbon with rum.

REPLACING THE ALCOHOL
Use apple juice or nondairy milk in place of the bourbon.

Bloody Mary Biscuits

Impress your guests at a brunch party with these out-of-the-ordinary spicy tomato biscuits! A small amount of vodka in the dough lends flakiness to the end result.

YIELD: 10 TO 12 BISCUITS

FOR THE BISCUITS:

2¼ CUPS (281 G) FLOUR

1½ TABLESPOONS (21 G) BAKING POWDER

¼ CUP (56 G) VEGAN MARGARINE

1 TABLESPOON (12.5 G) VEGAN SHORTENING

½ CUP (123 G) TOMATO SAUCE

1 TABLESPOON (15 ML) VODKA

2 TEASPOONS SOY SAUCE

1 TABLESPOON (15 ML) PICKLE JUICE OR LEMON JUICE

1 TEASPOON VEGAN WORCESTERSHIRE SAUCE

1 TEASPOON HOT SAUCE (OR TO TASTE)

1 TEASPOON CELERY SALT

FRESHLY GROUND BLACK PEPPER, TO TASTE

2 TABLESPOONS (30 G) CHOPPED DILL PICKLES

2 STRIPS VEGAN BACON, CHOPPED

3 TABLESPOONS (19 G) CHOPPED BLACK OR GREEN OLIVES

FOR GARNISH:

OLIVES, WHOLE

CHERRY TOMATOES, WHOLE

CELERY SLICES

DILL PICKLE SLICES

VEGAN BACON, COOKED, CUT INTO SMALL PIECES

To make the biscuits: Preheat oven to 400°F (200°C, or gas mark 6).

Mix the flour and baking powder together in a large mixing bowl. Begin cutting in the margarine and shortening with your fingers or a pastry knife, until it is incorporated into the dough and forms small pebbles.

Add the tomato sauce, vodka, soy sauce, pickle or lemon juice, Worcestershire sauce, hot sauce, celery salt, and pepper. Stir in the pickles, bacon, and olives, kneading them in if necessary.

Roll out dough into a 10 x 14-inch (25.4 x 35.5 cm) rectangle using a rolling pin on a floured surface. Fold in half and roll out again. Repeat 4 or 5 times. Roll out your final dough to about ¾ inch (2 cm) thick. Using a biscuit cutter or glass with a 2-inch (5 cm) diameter, cut out your biscuits and place on a prepared baking sheet. Re-roll your remaining dough and cut out more biscuits.

Bake the biscuits for 10 to 12 minutes, or until they've risen and the bottoms are golden.

To garnish: Skewer some olives, tomatoes, celery slices, dill pickle slices, and bits of vegan bacon on toothpicks or shortened wooden skewers, then insert your garnish into the top of each biscuit and serve!

RECIPE NOTE
Beware when using Worcestershire sauce, as most brands contain anchovies. Look for vegan Worcestershire at a natural foods store or well-stocked supermarket.

REPLACING THE ALCOHOL
Replace the vodka with water or nondairy milk.

Raspberry White Wine Doughnuts

If doughnuts are the new cupcake, they deserve a variety of flavors as well! These doughnuts showcase the delicate and classic combination of berries and white wine.

YIELD: 15 TO 18 DOUGHNUTS

FOR THE DOUGHNUTS:
1 TABLESPOON (8 G) CORNSTARCH
½ CUP (120 ML) ALMOND MILK
1 PACKAGE (9 G) YEAST
1 CUP (235 ML) ALMOND MILK, LUKEWARM
3 TABLESPOONS (38 G) VEGAN SHORTENING, MELTED
3 TABLESPOONS (42 G) VEGAN MARGARINE, MELTED
½ CUP (100 G) SUGAR
2 TABLESPOONS (30 G) BROWN SUGAR
4 CUPS (500 G) FLOUR
¼ TEASPOON SALT
VEGETABLE OIL, FOR FRYING

FOR THE GLAZE:
⅓ CUP (42 G) FRESH RASPBERRIES
2 TEASPOONS CORNSTARCH
½ CUP (120 ML) WHITE WINE
3 CUPS (360 G) POWDERED SUGAR

To make the doughnuts: In a small bowl, dissolve cornstarch in the milk, then microwave or cook on the stovetop in a saucepan over medium heat until thick. Set aside.

In a stand mixer equipped with a dough hook, or a large bowl, combine yeast with warm milk. Let sit until bubbles form, about 5 minutes.

Stir in the shortening and margarine. Add the sugar, brown sugar, and milk-cornstarch mixture, then stir to dissolve sugar.

Gradually add flour and salt and mix. Knead with the dough hook or by hand for 3 to 5 minutes, until the dough is smooth and forms a ball. Place the dough in a greased bowl, cover with a towel, and let rise for 1 hour, or until doubled in size.

Flour your workspace and roll dough ¾ inch (2 cm) thick. Create doughnuts with a 3-inch (7.5 cm) cookie or doughnut cutter and make holes in the centers with a smaller cookie cutter or your finger. Roll excess dough into doughnut holes. Cover doughnuts with a towel and let rise again for 40 minutes.

Prepare a deep fryer or a large pot with at least 2 inches (5 cm) of vegetable oil and heat to 350°F (180°C). Toss a small piece of dough in the oil. If the dough bubbles and rises to the top, the oil is ready.

Fry doughnuts 3 at a time for 1 minute on each side, or until golden, then transfer to a cooling rack with a baking sheet covered with paper towels or a paper bag below it to catch oil drips.

To make the glaze: Toss together raspberries and cornstarch in a saucepan. Add a splash of wine and turn heat to medium. Mash the raspberries as they cook. Stir until the mixture thickens, 3 to 4 minutes.

Remove from heat and add wine. Strain seeds out of mixture and return to the saucepan. Add powdered sugar and whisk until dissolved. Remove from heat.

Dunk doughnuts in glaze while they're still warm and return to wire rack to cool completely.

Apple Cider Doughnuts

An essential part of autumn, these are just like the spicy, flavorful doughnuts found at apple orchards.

YIELD: 12 DOUGHNUTS

FOR THE DOUGHNUTS:

2 SMALL APPLES, CHOPPED INTO ½-INCH
   (1.5 CM) PIECES

1 CUP (235 ML) APPLE CIDER

1 CINNAMON STICK

1½ CUPS (300 G) SUGAR

2 TABLESPOONS (25 G) VEGAN
   SHORTENING

2 TABLESPOONS (28 G) VEGAN
   MARGARINE

½ CUP (115 G) VANILLA-FLAVORED
   NONDAIRY YOGURT

1 TEASPOON VANILLA EXTRACT

4 CUPS (500 G) FLOUR

2 TEASPOONS BAKING POWDER

¼ TEASPOON BAKING SODA

2 TEASPOONS CINNAMON

¼ TEASPOON FRESHLY GRATED NUTMEG

½ TEASPOON SALT

VEGETABLE OIL, FOR FRYING

FOR THE GLAZE:

2 CUPS (240 G) POWDERED SUGAR

½ CUP (120 ML) APPLE CIDER, WARM

1 CUP (200 G) SUGAR

2 TEASPOONS CINNAMON

To make the doughnuts: Place apples, cider, and cinnamon stick in a saucepan over medium heat. Bring to a boil, then reduce the heat and simmer uncovered for 9 to 10 minutes. Remove from heat, remove cinnamon stick, and purée the apples, leaving a few chunks, to make 1 cup (245 g) of thick applesauce.

Cream together sugar, shortening, and margarine. Add applesauce, yogurt, and vanilla.

Combine flour, baking powder, baking soda, spices, and salt in a separate bowl. Gradually mix into the wet ingredients.

The dough should be very thick. A sticky dough won't hold its shape while frying, so if the dough seems watery or sticky, add flour ¼ cup (31 g) at a time until it reaches the right consistency.

Using a spatula, spread dough into a 10 x 14-inch (25.4 x 35.5 cm) rectangle that is about 1 inch (2.5 cm) thick onto a baking sheet lined with parchment, cover with plastic wrap, and chill for at least 2 hours.

Once the dough is chilled, prepare your deep fryer or large pot with at least 2 inches (5 cm) of vegetable oil and heat to 350°F (180°C). Toss a small piece of dough in the oil. If it bubbles and rises to the top, the oil is ready.

Cut out doughnuts with a 3-inch (7.5 cm) cookie or doughnut cutter and make holes in the centers with a smaller cookie cutter or your finger. Fry 2 or 3 doughnuts at a time for 1 to 2 minutes on each side until golden. Transfer to a wire rack set over a baking sheet lined with paper towels or paper bags to catch oil drips.

To make the glaze: Stir the powdered sugar with the cider in a small bowl, whisking until it forms a smooth glaze.

Combine the sugar and cinnamon in a shallow bowl. Submerge doughnuts in the glaze and let the excess drip off, then transfer to cinnamon sugar mixture and coat completely.

> **RECIPE NOTE**
> Doughnuts taste best the day they're made, but will keep for 3 to 4 days when stored in an airtight container.

Kahlúa Chocolate Doughnuts

Already love at first bite, Kahlúa and chocolate make an appearance in this decadent, double-dipped doughnut.

YIELD: 15 TO 18 DOUGHNUTS

FOR THE DOUGHNUTS:

½ CUP (120 ML) ALMOND MILK PLUS
    1 TABLESPOON (8 G) CORNSTARCH
¾ CUP (180 ML) ALMOND MILK,
    LUKEWARM
1 PACKAGE (9 G) YEAST
¼ CUP (60 ML) KAHLÚA OR OTHER
    COFFEE LIQUEUR
3 TABLESPOONS (38 G) VEGAN
    SHORTENING, MELTED
3 TABLESPOONS (42 G) VEGAN
    MARGARINE, MELTED
½ CUP (100 G) SUGAR
2 TABLESPOONS (30 G) BROWN SUGAR
¾ CUP (88.5 G) COCOA POWDER
3¼ CUPS (406 G) FLOUR
¼ TEASPOON SALT
VEGETABLE OIL FOR FRYING

FOR THE GLAZE:

3 CUPS (360 G) POWDERED SUGAR
¼ CUP (60 ML) NONDAIRY MILK, HEATED
¼ CUP (60 ML) KAHLÚA OR OTHER
    COFFEE LIQUEUR
1 TEASPOON VANILLA EXTRACT

FOR THE GANACHE:

2 CUPS (350 G) VEGAN CHOCOLATE CHIPS
⅓ CUP (80 ML) SOY CREAMER
1 TABLESPOON (15 ML) KAHLÚA OR
    OTHER COFFEE LIQUEUR

To make the doughnuts: In a small bowl, stir cornstarch in ½ cup (120 ml) almond milk, then microwave or cook on stovetop in a saucepan over medium heat until thick. Set aside.

In a stand mixer equipped with a dough hook, or a large mixing bowl, combine the lukewarm milk with the package of yeast. Let sit until bubbles form, about 5 minutes.

Stir Kahlúa, shortening, and margarine into the milk-yeast mixture. Stir in sugar, brown sugar, and milk-cornstarch mixture.

Gradually mix in cocoa powder, flour, and salt. Knead with dough hook or by hand, 3 to 5 minutes, until dough is smooth and forms a ball. Place the dough in a greased bowl, cover with a towel, and let rise for 1 hour or until dough has doubled in size.

Flour your workspace and roll dough ¾ inch (2 cm) thick. Create doughnuts with a 3-inch (7.5 cm) cookie or doughnut cutter and make holes in the centers with a smaller cookie cutter or your finger. Roll excess dough into doughnut holes. Cover doughnuts with a towel and let rise again for 40 minutes.

Prepare deep fryer or large pot with at least 2 inches (5 cm) of vegetable oil and heat to 350°F (180°C). Toss a small piece of dough in the oil. If it bubbles and rises to the top, the oil is ready.

Fry doughnuts 3 at a time for 1 minute on each side, or until golden, then transfer to a cooling rack with a cookie sheet lined with paper towels or a paper bag below it to catch oil drips.

To make the glaze: Whisk powdered sugar into the milk until dissolved. Stir in the Kahlúa and vanilla extract. Dunk each doughnut in the glaze, then return to the cooling rack and let set.

To make the ganache: Melt chocolate with creamer, then stir in Kahlúa. Dip doughnut tops in ganache.

Strawberry Mimosa Muffin Tops

Muffin tops rose to fame after endless pop culture references, and they undoubtedly remain a tasty brunch item. Even though we learned from *Seinfeld* that you have to make the whole muffin first, this recipe makes just the muffin top. The Champagne glaze probably resolves that offense, though.

YIELD: 8 MUFFIN TOPS

FOR THE MUFFIN TOPS:

3 CUPS (375 G) FLOUR

1½ TABLESPOONS (20.5 G) BAKING POWDER

¼ TEASPOON SALT

½ CUP (100 G) SUGAR

½ CUP (112 G) VEGAN MARGARINE

½ CUP (120 ML) CHAMPAGNE

¼ CUP (60 ML) ORANGE JUICE

⅓ CUP (77 G) VANILLA- OR STRAWBERRY-FLAVORED NONDAIRY YOGURT

2 TEASPOONS ORANGE ZEST

½ TEASPOON VANILLA EXTRACT

½ CUP (85 G) SLICED STRAWBERRIES

FOR THE GLAZE:

2 TABLESPOONS (30 G) CHAMPAGNE

1¼ CUPS (150 G) POWDERED SUGAR

To make the muffin tops: Preheat oven to 400°F (200°C, or gas mark 6).

Sift together flour, baking powder, salt, and sugar. Cut in margarine with your fingers or a pastry cutter and evenly distribute through the dry ingredients until it forms coarse pebbles.

Add Champagne, orange juice, yogurt, orange zest, and vanilla extract. Mix until almost combined, then add in strawberries and finish mixing. The dough should be thick and somewhat sticky.

Using a large (¼ cup, or 60 ml) cookie scoop or ice cream scoop, drop batter onto a parchment-lined cookie sheet. You should have enough batter for about 8 muffin tops.

Bake for 16 to 18 minutes, or until the tops are firm and look a bit crunchy. Let cool on the cookie sheet for a few minutes, then transfer to a wire rack.

To make the glaze: Stir together Champagne and powdered sugar until completely smooth. The glaze should be thick but pourable.

Drizzle glaze onto cooled muffin tops. If the pastry is absorbing the glaze, it's too thin. Add more powdered sugar and continue glazing. Let the glaze set before eating.

Apple Cider Cinnamon Rolls

This recipe is a cross between apple pie, cinnamon rolls, and apple cider dough-nuts, topped off with an apple rum glaze. It's a perfect breakfast treat in the fall.

YIELD: 12 TO 14 ROLLS

FOR THE DOUGH:

1 CUP (235 ML) APPLE CIDER, WARM
1 PACKAGE (9 G) YEAST
½ CUP (125 G) APPLESAUCE
¼ CUP (50 G) SUGAR
⅓ CUP (75 G) VEGAN MARGARINE OR
   COCONUT OIL, MELTED
1 TEASPOON LEMON ZEST
3½ CUPS (438 G) FLOUR
1½ TEASPOONS CINNAMON
¼ TEASPOON FRESHLY GRATED NUTMEG
⅛ TEASPOON GROUND CLOVES
⅛ TEASPOON GROUND CARDAMOM
½ TEASPOON SALT

FOR THE FILLING:

3 TABLESPOONS (42 G) VEGAN MARGARINE
   OR COCONUT OIL, DIVIDED
2 MEDIUM APPLES, PEELED AND DICED
2 TEASPOONS CORNSTARCH
1 TEASPOON CINNAMON
½ CUP (115 G) BROWN SUGAR, DIVIDED
¼ CUP (50 G) SUGAR
1 TABLESPOON (7 G) CINNAMON

FOR THE GLAZE:

1 TABLESPOON (15 ML) APPLE CIDER
1 TABLESPOON (15 ML) RUM
1 TABLESPOON (14 G) VEGAN MARGA-
   RINE, MELTED
1¼ CUPS (150 G) POWDERED SUGAR

Line a 9 x 13-inch (23 x 33 cm) baking pan with parchment.

To make the dough: Combine cider and yeast in a large bowl or stand mixer and let stand until bubbles form. Add applesauce, sugar, margarine or oil, and lemon zest and stir until combined.

Stir in the flour, spices, and salt. Knead for 10 minutes, forming dough into a ball. Place dough in a greased bowl, cover with a towel, and let rise in a warm place for 1 hour, or until doubled in size.

To make the filling: Melt 1 tablespoon (14 g) margarine in a saucepan over medium heat. Add chopped apples, cornstarch, cinnamon, and ¼ cup (60 g) brown sugar. Stir until the sugar dis-solves, the syrup thickens, and the apples soften, 3 to 4 minutes. Remove from heat and let cool.

Punch down risen dough. Sprinkle countertop with flour.

Roll dough into a 10 x 14-inch (25.5 x 35.5 cm) rectangle, with the long edge facing you. Spread remaining 2 tablespoons (28 g) margarine over the dough, then sprinkle on the sugar, remaining ¼ cup (60 g) brown sugar, and cinnamon. Spoon half of the apple mixture onto the dough and roll up tightly. Seam facing down, slice the roll into 12 to 14 pieces. Place the rolls face up in the prepared pan with the sides touching, and spoon the rest of the apple mixture on top.

Cover pan with a towel and let rise for 20 minutes. In the mean-time, preheat oven to 375°F (190°C, or gas mark 5).

Bake for 20 to 25 minutes until golden. Let cool for 10 minutes.

To make the glaze: Combine cider, rum, and margarine in a bowl. Stir in powdered sugar until smooth. Drizzle glaze on rolls and let set.

CHAPTER 3

the café

Lattes, espresso, and hot tea are served up in dessert form! Get your caffeine buzz from brownies and cupcakes, then enjoy the delicate, soothing flavors of tea with lavish baked goods like biscotti, baklava, and bread.

Horchata Cookies

Common in Latin countries, horchata is a cool rice drink infused with cinnamon, almonds, and lime. It can be found in grocery stores near the shelf-stable soy and nut milks or in Mexican markets. Earthy almonds contrast with the bright flavor of lime, just as spicy cinnamon marries with the refreshing qualities of horchata.

YIELD: 18 COOKIES

FOR THE COOKIES:

⅓ CUP (80 ML) ALMOND MILK OR
   PREPARED HORCHATA

1 TABLESPOON (7 G) GROUND FLAX SEED

⅓ CUP (80 ML) CANOLA OIL

½ CUP (100 G) SUGAR

¼ CUP (60 G) LIGHT BROWN SUGAR

1 TEASPOON LIME ZEST

1 TABLESPOON (15 ML) LIME JUICE

¾ TEASPOON VANILLA EXTRACT

2 CUPS (250 ML) FLOUR

3 TABLESPOONS (23 G) WHITE RICE
   FLOUR

1 TEASPOON BAKING SODA

¼ TEASPOON SALT

½ TEASPOON CINNAMON

¼ CUP (24 G) GROUND ROASTED
   ALMONDS

1 CUP (110 G) CHOPPED ROASTED
   ALMONDS, DIVIDED

FOR THE GLAZE:

¾ CUP (90 G) POWDERED SUGAR

1 TEASPOON LIME ZEST

2 TABLESPOONS (30 ML) LIME JUICE

To make the cookies: Preheat oven to 350°F (180°C, or gas mark 4).

Whisk together the almond milk and ground flax seed.

In a large bowl, stir together the oil, sugars, lime zest and juice, vanilla extract, and almond milk/flax seed mixture. Sift in the flour, rice flour, baking soda, salt, and cinnamon. Stir until just combined.

Add the ground roasted almonds and ⅔ cup (73 g) of the chopped roasted almonds to the dough and mix until incorporated. Reserve the remaining ⅓ cup (37 g) of the chopped almonds for garnish.

Roll golf ball–sized pieces of dough into balls. Flatten on a prepared cookie sheet, then bake for 10 to 12 minutes. Let cool on the tray for a few minutes, then transfer to a wire rack to cool completely.

To make the glaze: Combine powdered sugar and lime zest and juice, and stir until the powdered sugar is dissolved. Drizzle the glaze on the cooled cookies. Sprinkle some of the reserved chopped nuts on top of each glazed cookie. Let the glaze set, then serve. Store in an airtight container for up to 1 week.

RECIPE NOTE
Either buy roasted almonds and chop/grind them, or roast your own! Scatter 1½ cups (217.5 g) whole almonds on a cookie sheet and place in a 350°F (180°C, or gas mark 4) oven for 10 minutes, or until fragrant. Let cool, then chop in a food processor. Remove 1 cup (73 g) for the recipe, then grind the rest (you'll need ¼ cup ground).

Coconut Hot Chocolate Fudge

This fudge takes a little more time than your average fudge, but it's beyond average with its smooth texture and rich gourmet chocolate taste. Because it calls for coconut oil and coconut milk instead of margarine and soy milk, it's soy-free as well!

YIELD: 60 TO 72 ONE INCH (2.5 CM) SERVINGS

2¾ CUPS (450 G) SUGAR
⅔ CUP (79 G) COCOA POWDER
3 TABLESPOONS (42 G) VIRGIN
   COCONUT OIL
1 TABLESPOON (15 ML) AGAVE NECTAR
1 CUP (235 ML) COCONUT MILK
½ TEASPOON COCONUT EXTRACT
1 TEASPOON VANILLA EXTRACT

Combine all ingredients except the extracts in a medium-large saucepan.

Cook over medium heat until the sugar dissolves, then bring to a boil. Reduce heat to medium-low and place the lid on the saucepan. Cook for 3 minutes.

Remove lid and cook to 238°F (114°C) or when a spoonful of the mixture dropped into a cup of cold water holds its shape and is pliable and squishy, which will take about 15 to 20 minutes, stirring frequently.

Turn off heat and let mixture cool to 110°F (43°C), about 40 minutes, then add the coconut and vanilla extracts. Stir the mixture with a wooden spoon for a couple of minutes.

Pour into a parchment-lined 8-inch (20.5 cm) square pan. If the fudge starts to solidify while pouring, moisten your hands and press down the fudge. Let cool, cut into small squares, and eat!

Chipotle Lime Hot Chocolate Fudge Cookies

Chipotle adds a deep, rich, smoky flavor to standard Mexican hot chocolate. These flavors nestle sweetly into a canvas of fudgy chocolate cookie, complemented with the fresh taste of lime.

YIELD: 18 TO 20 COOKIES

½ CUP (87 G) PLUS ⅔ CUP (117 G) VEGAN
   CHOCOLATE CHIPS, DIVIDED
½ CUP (120 ML) NONDAIRY MILK
½ CUP (112 G) COCONUT OIL
2 TEASPOONS VANILLA EXTRACT
1⅓ CUPS (233 G) SUGAR
2 TABLESPOONS (16 G) CORNSTARCH
1½ TEASPOONS GROUND CHIPOTLE
⅛ TEASPOON CINNAMON
2 TEASPOONS LIME ZEST
2 CUPS (250 G) FLOUR
⅔ CUP (79 G) COCOA
2 TEASPOONS BAKING POWDER
¼ TEASPOON SALT

Preheat oven to 350°F (180°C, or gas mark 4).

Melt the ½ cup of chocolate chips with about ⅓ cup (80 ml) of the milk. Pour the melted chocolate and milk into a large bowl, then add the rest of the milk, coconut oil, vanilla, sugar, cornstarch, chipotle, cinnamon, and lime zest.

Add the flour (not sifted), cocoa, baking powder, and salt. Stir until thoroughly combined, then mix in the ⅔ cup chocolate chips.

Spoon out golf ball–sized portions of dough and flatten them to about ½ inch (1.5 cm) on a cookie sheet lined with parchment paper.

Bake for 13 to 15 minutes or until the edges are very firm and the centers look chewy and feel soft to the touch. Let rest on the cookie sheet for a minute or so, then carefully transfer to a cooling rack.

RECIPE NOTE
Coconut oil can be pricey, so replace half with canola oil if you'd like.

Lemon Espresso Shortbread

The body of this crisp, flavorful shortbread encapsulates the richness of espresso, accented with fresh lemon zest. Espresso is sometimes served with a bit of lemon zest, as the bright citrus flavor cuts through the bitterness of the coffee.

YIELD: 30 COOKIES

¾ CUP (169 G) VEGAN MARGARINE
¾ CUP (90 G) POWDERED SUGAR
4 TEASPOONS GROUND ESPRESSO BEANS
½ TEASPOON VANILLA EXTRACT
1 TABLESPOON (15 ML) MAPLE SYRUP
1 TABLESPOON (6 G) LEMON ZEST
¼ TEASPOON SALT
2 CUPS (250 G) FLOUR

Cream together the margarine, powdered sugar, coffee, vanilla extract, maple syrup, lemon zest, and salt in a large bowl with electric beaters.

Gradually sift in the flour and stir after each addition until a dough forms.

Transfer dough to a gallon-sized resealable plastic bag. Keeping the bag unsealed, use a rolling pin to flatten the dough evenly, making sure to spread it to the bottom corners, then working your way up to the open end. The dough should nearly fill the bag, and should only be about ⅛ inch (.5 cm) thick.

Refrigerate the rolled-out dough (making sure to keep it flat) for about 30 minutes.

Preheat oven to 350°F (180°C, or gas mark 4).

Cut the plastic bag open along the seams and turn the dough onto a cutting board. Using a sharp knife, trim off any rough edges, then run your knife through the dough vertically and horizontally, making about thirty 2-inch (5 cm) squares.

Place on a lightly oiled or parchment-lined baking sheet and bake for 12 to 15 minutes, or until the edges are crispy and the centers are firm but not burned.

RECIPE NOTE
If you don't have ground espresso beans, swap them out for regular ground coffee.

Butterscotch Mocha Brownies with Caramel Almond Topping

This mocha butterscotch brownie is topped with a swirl of sweet butterscotch frosting and buttery caramel, then garnished with almond praline, satisfying even the sweetest of teeth.

YIELD: 9 BROWNIES

FOR THE BROWNIES:
1¾ CUPS (219 G) FLOUR
⅔ CUP (79 G) COCOA POWDER
2 TEASPOONS BAKING POWDER
1 TABLESPOON (8 G) CORNSTARCH
1½ TEASPOONS GROUND COFFEE BEANS
½ TEASPOON SALT
PINCH OF CINNAMON
1½ CUPS (300 G) SUGAR
½ CUP (120 ML) CANOLA OIL
⅔ CUP (117 G) VEGAN CHOCOLATE CHIPS,
   MELTED
1 TEASPOON VANILLA EXTRACT
½ TEASPOON BUTTERSCOTCH EXTRACT
⅔ CUP (160 ML) ALMOND MILK

FOR THE CARAMEL:
⅔ CUP (150 G) BROWN SUGAR
½ CUP (120 ML) ALMOND MILK
1½ TABLESPOONS (12 G) CORNSTARCH
1 TABLESPOON (15 ML) WATER
⅛ TEASPOON BUTTERSCOTCH EXTRACT
¼ CUP (56 G) VEGAN MARGARINE
1 TEASPOON (5 ML) VANILLA EXTRACT

FOR THE TOPPING:
BUTTERSCOTCH BUTTERCREAM
   (PAGE 168)
⅓ CUP (48 ML) WHOLE TOASTED
   ALMONDS

To make the brownies: Preheat oven to 350°F (180°C, or gas mark 4). Prepare an 8-inch (20.5 cm) square pan by greasing it or lining it with parchment paper.

In a medium bowl, sift together the flour, cocoa powder, baking powder, cornstarch, coffee, salt, and cinnamon. Set aside.

In a large bowl, stir together the sugar, canola oil, chocolate chips, vanilla extract, butterscotch extract, and milk.

Gradually add the dry ingredient mixture to the wet ingredients, stirring after each addition until smooth and thick. Pour into prepared pan and bake for 25 to 30 minutes. Let cool, then cut into squares.

To make the caramel: In a saucepan over medium heat, combine the brown sugar and milk. Stir constantly until the sugar dissolves and the mixture begins to thicken, 10 to 12 minutes.

In a separate bowl, dissolve the cornstarch in the water, then add to the sugar mixture. Stir constantly until the caramel thickens, and cook for 2 more minutes. Remove from heat and stir in butterscotch extract, margarine, and vanilla.

Top each brownie with a dollop of buttercream and about 2 teaspoons (10 ml) caramel. Stir almonds into the remaining caramel. Return the saucepan to the stove and heat for 3 to 5 minutes, stirring constantly. Garnish each brownie with the caramel-covered almonds.

> **RECIPE NOTE**
> Add 1 tablespoon (15 ml) bourbon or brandy to the Butterscotch Buttercream, if desired.

Espresso Fudge Cupcakes

Chocolate and coffee are one of those made-in-heaven culinary pairings, like wine and cheese or peanut butter and jelly. This rich, fudgy, coffee-infused cupcake keeps it simple and classy.

YIELD: 12 CUPCAKES

FOR THE CUPCAKES:
½ CUP (112 G) VEGAN MARGARINE
¾ CUP (150 G) SUGAR
½ CUP (115 G) NONDAIRY YOGURT
¼ CUP (60 ML) NONDAIRY MILK
¼ CUP (44 G) VEGAN CHOCOLATE CHIPS, MELTED
½ CUP (120 ML) STRONG BREWED COFFEE
1½ TEASPOONS VANILLA EXTRACT
1¼ CUPS (156 G) FLOUR
½ CUP (59 G) COCOA POWDER
2 TEASPOONS BAKING POWDER
¼ TEASPOON SALT
4 TEASPOONS FINELY GROUND COFFEE BEANS
COFFEE BUTTERCREAM (PAGE 168)

FOR THE GARNISH (OPTIONAL):
COFFEE BEANS, WHOLE
VEGAN CHOCOLATE CHIPS
VEGAN CHOCOLATE CURLS
CINNAMON

To make the cupcakes: Preheat oven to 350°F (180°C, or gas mark 4).

Cream together the margarine and sugar. Add the yogurt, milk, chocolate chips, brewed coffee, and vanilla extract. Continue beating until fluffy.

Sift in the flour, cocoa powder, baking powder, salt, and ground coffee and continue mixing until just combined.

Line a cupcake pan with 12 liners. Fill each cup halfway with batter. Bake for 18 to 20 minutes or until firm in the center. Transfer to a cooling rack.

Top cupcakes with Coffee Buttercream using a knife or pastry bag.

To garnish: Sprinkle each cupcake with coffee beans, chocolate chips, chocolate curls, and cinnamon.

Coffee Ice Cream

I created this recipe for straight-up coffee ice cream because you'll rarely find a vegan version in stores. A smidge of chocolate, salt, and vanilla create depth in the flavor, but the coffee shines in this dessert.

YIELD: 1 PINT (285 G)

3 TABLESPOONS (12 G) COFFEE BEANS
1 CAN (15 OUNCES OR 450 ML) COCONUT MILK
½ CUP (100 G) SUGAR
½ CUP (120 ML) ALMOND MILK
1 TEASPOON VANILLA EXTRACT
¾ TEASPOON COFFEE EXTRACT (OPTIONAL)
½ TEASPOON CHOCOLATE EXTRACT OR COCOA POWDER
1/8 TEASPOON SALT

Coarsely grind the coffee beans.

Combine the coconut milk and beans in a medium saucepan over medium-high heat. Bring to a boil and let boil for 7 to 8 minutes.

Add the sugar and stir until it dissolves completely, and continue to boil for 4 more minutes. Turn off the heat and stir in the almond milk. Add the extracts and salt.

Let the mixture cool for about 15 minutes. Strain the mixture to remove the large chunks of coffee beans.

Freeze in ice cream maker according to manufacturer's instructions.

Mexican Coffee Truffles ▶

Rich chocolate truffles with a coconut milk base are infused with sweet cinnamon and coffee liqueur.

YIELD: 20 TO 24 TRUFFLES

1/3 CUP (80 ML) FULL-FAT COCONUT MILK
1 PACKAGE (12 OUNCES OR 340 G) VEGAN SEMISWEET CHOCOLATE CHIPS
¼ CUP (30 G) COCOA POWDER
¼ TEASPOON CINNAMON
3 TABLESPOONS (45 ML) COFFEE LIQUEUR
1 TABLESPOON (15 ML) TEQUILA
1 TEASPOON COFFEE EXTRACT
COCOA POWDER, FOR ROLLING

Melt the coconut milk and chocolate chips together in a double boiler over medium heat, or melt in a glass bowl in the microwave. Stir until smooth.

Add the cocoa powder, cinnamon, coffee liqueur, tequila, and coffee extract. Cover and chill in the refrigerator for at least 5 to 6 hours, or overnight.

Sprinkle a layer of cocoa powder on a plate for rolling truffles. Remove truffle mix from refrigerator.

Using a small (1 tablespoon, or 15 ml) cookie scoop or a 1-tablespoon (15 ml) measuring spoon, scoop out chocolate and roll into balls. Roll in the cocoa to coat. Set on a serving tray or in mini cupcake liners. Store in the refrigerator until ready to serve.

RECIPE NOTE
You can also add other ingredients to give the coating extra flavor and texture, such as a sprinkle of cinnamon, a spoonful of freshly ground coffee beans, or gold luster dust for a glittery sheen (if that's how you roll).

Irish Coffee Pudding Pie

This chocolate pudding pie infused with Irish whiskey and coffee is simple and decadent.

YIELD: 12 SERVINGS

FOR THE CRUST:

1¾ CUPS (205 G) CHOCOLATE COOKIE CRUMBS

3 TABLESPOONS (52 G) VEGAN MARGARINE, MELTED

2 TABLESPOONS (30 ML) AGAVE NECTAR

2 TEASPOONS GROUND COFFEE BEANS

1 TO 2 TABLESPOONS (15 TO 30 ML) IRISH WHISKEY

FOR THE FILLING:

1¾ CUPS (411 ML) NONDAIRY MILK

¾ CUP (175 ML) STRONG BREWED COFFEE

¼ CUP (30 G) COCOA POWDER

½ CUP (100 G) SUGAR

3 TABLESPOONS (24 G) CORNSTARCH

¼ TEASPOON AGAR POWDER

¼ TEASPOON SALT

½ CUP (88 G) VEGAN CHOCOLATE CHIPS

¼ CUP (60 ML) IRISH WHISKEY

1½ TEASPOONS VANILLA EXTRACT

1½ TEASPOONS COFFEE EXTRACT

VEGAN WHIPPED CREAM (OPTIONAL)

To make the crust: Preheat oven to 350°F (180°C, or gas mark 4).

Stir together all crust ingredients in a small bowl, adding more whiskey or a splash of nondairy milk if the mixture is too crumbly.

Coat a 9-inch (23 cm) pie plate or tin with cooking spray or vegetable oil. Spoon the cookie crumb mixture into the plate, then press evenly, using a spoon to smooth it out. Make sure the edges of the pie plate are covered and even. Bake for 10 minutes, or until firm. Set aside to cool.

To make the filling: Combine milk, coffee, cocoa powder, sugar, cornstarch, agar, and salt in a medium-sized saucepan and whisk until smooth.

Turn the heat on to medium-high and bring to a low boil. Cook for 8 to 9 minutes, stirring constantly.

Once the pudding is very thick, remove from heat and stir in the chocolate chips until melted. Let cool for 2 to 3 minutes.

Add the whiskey and extracts, mixing in completely. Pour the pudding into the crust. Eat any leftovers as regular pudding.

Let the pie cool completely on the stove, then store covered in the refrigerator. Eat topped with whipped cream, if desired.

REPLACING THE ALCOHOL
You can swap the whiskey for more coffee or nondairy milk, but the pie will no longer be Irish.

Pumpkin Latte Cheesecake

Re-create the seasonal lattes in pie form at home!

YIELD: 12 SERVINGS

FOR THE CRUST:

1¾ CUPS (205 G) CHOCOLATE COOKIE CRUMBS

¼ CUP (56 G) VEGAN MARGARINE, MELTED

3 TABLESPOONS (45 G) PACKED BROWN SUGAR

1 TABLESPOON (7 G) GROUND COFFEE BEANS

½ TEASPOON CINNAMON

⅛ TEASPOON FRESHLY GRATED NUTMEG

⅛ TEASPOON GROUND GINGER

⅛ TEASPOON ALLSPICE

⅛ TEASPOON GROUND CLOVES

¼ TEASPOON SALT

½ TEASPOON COFFEE EXTRACT (OPTIONAL)

2 TO 3 TABLESPOONS (30 TO 45 ML) NONDAIRY MILK

FOR THE FILLING:

¼ CUP (60 ML) NONDAIRY MILK

½ CUP (120 ML) STRONG BREWED COFFEE

1 CUP (245 G) PUMPKIN PURÉE

2 TEASPOONS COFFEE EXTRACT

2 TEASPOONS CINNAMON

¼ TEASPOON GROUND GINGER

¼ TEASPOON FRESHLY GRATED NUTMEG

¼ TEASPOON ALLSPICE

PINCH OF GROUND CLOVES

2 TABLESPOONS (30 ML) LEMON JUICE

⅓ CUP (43 G) CORNSTARCH OR ARROWROOT POWDER

1 TEASPOON AGAR POWDER

¾ CUP (150 G) SUGAR

PINCH OF SALT

8 OUNCES (227 G) VEGAN CREAM CHEESE (1 TUB), SOFTENED

To make the crust: Preheat oven to 350°F (180°C, or gas mark 4).

Stir together all crust ingredients in a small bowl, adding more nondairy milk if the mixture is crumbly.

Coat a 9-inch (23 cm) pie plate or tin with cooking spray or vegetable oil. Spoon the cookie crumb mixture into the plate, then press evenly into the plate, using a spoon to smooth it out. Make sure the edges are covered and even. Bake for 10 minutes, or until firm. Set aside to cool.

To make the filling: Combine all the filling ingredients except the cream cheese in a medium saucepan and whisk to dissolve the cornstarch. Turn the heat to medium and continue whisking. Stir frequently until very thick, about 6 minutes.

Turn off the heat, then stir in the cream cheese until smooth.

Let sit for a minute, then pour into prepared crust. Let cool on the stove or a cooling rack. Cover and transfer to the refrigerator for at least 3 to 4 hours.

RECIPE NOTES
- If you can't find coffee extract, replace 2 to 3 tablespoons (30 to 45 g) of the coffee with a shot of espresso (home brewed, or bought from a coffee shop).
- You can replace the cinnamon, allspice, ginger, nutmeg, and cloves in the crust with 1 teaspoon pumpkin pie spice.

Rosy Peach and Green Tea Ice Cream

Matcha is a concentrated and flavorful Japanese green tea powder, which makes it a great ingredient for baking. Matcha, rose, and peach combine in this ice cream as a trifecta of delicate flavors that work beautifully together. The strength of flavor in rosewater greatly varies from brand to brand, so pick one that suits your taste.

YIELD: 1 PINT (285 G)

1 CUP (235 ML) ALMOND MILK
1 CUP (235 ML) COCONUT MILK OR
   CREAMER
⅔ CUP (133 G) SUGAR
2 TEASPOONS MATCHA POWDER
1 TEASPOON ROSEWATER
1 TEASPOON VANILLA EXTRACT (OMIT IF
   USING VANILLA-FLAVORED COCONUT
   CREAMER)
2 MEDIUM-LARGE PEACHES

Combine all ingredients except for the peaches in a small saucepan.

Bring to a boil over medium-high heat, whisking frequently to dissolve the matcha and sugar. Remove from heat. Peel the peaches. Purée one of the peaches and stir into the mixture.

Freeze in an ice cream maker according to manufacturer's instructions. Chop the other peach and add to the ice cream according to the manufacturer's instructions.

RECIPE NOTES
- If using concentrated rosewater made from rose oil, 1 teaspoon will be plenty. You may have to use up to a tablespoon with diluted rosewater. Do a taste test, then adjust flavors as needed.
- Add an additional 2 tablespoons (26 g) sugar if using coconut milk instead of coconut creamer.

Cherry Chia Kombucha Margarita

This is a fusion of two tasty drinks: kombucha and margaritas.

YIELD: 2 SERVINGS

SALT, FOR GLASSES
3 LIME WEDGES
¼ CUP (60 ML) LIME JUICE
2 TABLESPOONS (30 ML) AGAVE NECTAR
2 OUNCES (60 ML) TRIPLE SEC OR OTHER
   ORANGE LIQUEUR
3 OUNCES (90 ML) TEQUILA
1 CUP (235 ML) STORE-BOUGHT CHERRY
   CHIA KOMBUCHA

Fill a plate or saucer with salt. Rub a lime wedge around the rims of 2 margarita glasses, then roll the outer edges of the glasses in the salt, gently tapping off any excess.

Combine the lime juice, agave nectar, triple sec, and tequila in a cocktail shaker (or other cup with a lid) filled with ice. Gently shake until all the ingredients are thoroughly mixed, then strain into the glasses. Stir half of the kombucha into each glass and garnish with a lime wedge.

REPLACING THE ALCOHOL
Use orange juice instead of triple sec and add more kombucha instead of tequila.

Lavender Mint Tea Cookies

Herbal tea finds a home with fresh mint in these sumptuous shortbread cookies.

YIELD: 30 COOKIES

¾ CUP (168 G) VEGAN MARGARINE

¼ CUP (60 ML) CANOLA OIL

1¼ CUPS (150 G) POWDERED SUGAR

2 TABLESPOONS (30 G) LIME JUICE

2 TEASPOONS VANILLA EXTRACT

4 TEASPOONS FINELY CHOPPED
   FRESH MINT LEAVES

2½ TEASPOONS CULINARY LAVENDER,
   CRUSHED

2¼ CUPS (281 G) FLOUR

¼ TEASPOON BAKING SODA

¼ TEASPOON BAKING POWDER

¼ TEASPOON SALT

Preheat oven to 350°F (180°C, or gas mark 4).

In a large bowl or stand mixer, beat together margarine and canola oil. Add powdered sugar, and beat the mixture to a smooth and airy consistency.

Add the lime juice, vanilla extract, chopped mint, and lavender buds, and mix until all the ingredients are incorporated.

Sift in flour, baking soda, baking powder, and salt, and mix until smooth. Drop by tablespoonfuls onto a parchment-lined baking sheet and bake for 11 to 13 minutes, or until the edges are lightly golden.

Transfer to a cooling rack and let cool completely. Store in an airtight container for up to 2 weeks.

Butterscotch Amaretto Biscotti

Amaretto, toasted almonds, and butterscotch intertwine in unassuming biscotti for a flavorful treat that pairs well with tea.

YIELD: 24 BISCOTTI

½ CUP (55 G) SLICED RAW ALMONDS, DIVIDED

½ CUP (112 G) VEGAN MARGARINE

½ CUP (100 G) SUGAR

¼ CUP (60 G) BROWN SUGAR

¼ CUP (60 ML) AMARETTO

1 TO 2 TABLESPOONS (15 TO 20 ML) NON-DAIRY MILK

½ TEASPOON VANILLA EXTRACT

½ TEASPOON ALMOND EXTRACT

2 CUPS (250 G) FLOUR

1½ TEASPOONS BAKING POWDER

¼ TEASPOON SALT

¼ CUP (44 G) VEGAN BUTTERSCOTCH CHIPS

Preheat oven to 325°F (170°C, or gas mark 3).

Spread ¼ (27.5 g) cup sliced almonds on a baking sheet lined with parchment paper and toast until golden and fragrant, 4 to 5 minutes. Remove from the oven and set aside.

Cream together margarine, sugar, and brown sugar. Add the amaretto, 1 tablespoon milk, and extracts and mix until smooth.

Sift in the flour, baking powder, and salt and mix until halfway combined. Add the remaining ¼ cup (27.5 g) toasted almonds and butterscotch chips. Mix until completely combined. If the dough is crumbly, add the additional tablespoon of milk.

Form the dough into a 3-inch (7.5 cm) wide, 12-inch (30.5 cm) long, and 1-inch (2.5 cm) thick loaf. Press the ¼ cup untoasted almonds evenly on top of the loaf. Bake on the parchment-lined cookie sheet used for the almonds for about 35 minutes, or until golden with a firm center.

Let cool for 10 to 15 minutes, then slice into ½-inch (1.5 cm) wedges. Line them out on the cookie sheet and bake for 5 more minutes on each side.

RECIPE NOTE

Dress up the biscotti with a butterscotch drizzle, if desired. Melt 1 cup (176 g) vegan butterscotch chips with 1 tablespoon (12.5 g) vegan shortening in the microwave, or stovetop double boiler over medium heat. Drizzle a spoonful of melted butterscotch over each biscotti.

Chocolate Chai Biscotti

Chai spice tea leaves are ground up and added directly to the batter for a rich, flavorful chai cookie.

YIELD: 24 BISCOTTI

FOR THE BISCOTTI:

½ CUP (112 G) VEGAN MARGARINE
1 CUP (200 G) SUGAR
⅓ CUP (80 ML) NONDAIRY MILK
¾ TEASPOON VANILLA EXTRACT
1¼ CUPS (156 G) FLOUR
½ CUP (59 G) COCOA POWDER
2 TEASPOONS CHAI TEA, GROUND
1½ TEASPOONS BAKING POWDER
¼ TEASPOON SALT

FOR THE DRIZZLE:

1½ CUPS (263 G) CHOCOLATE CHIPS
1 TABLESPOON (12.5 G) VEGAN
   SHORTENING
COARSE SUGAR

To make the biscotti: Preheat oven to 325°F (170°C, or gas mark 3).

Cream together margarine, sugar, milk, and vanilla extract. Add the flour, cocoa, chai powder, baking powder, and salt.

Form the dough into a 3-inch (7.5 cm) wide, 12-inch (30.5 cm) long, and 1-inch (2.5 cm) thick loaf. Bake on a parchment-lined cookie sheet for 30 minutes.

Let cool for 10 to 15 minutes, then slice into ½-inch (1.5 cm) wedges and bake for 6 to 8 more minutes on each side.

To make the drizzle: Melt chocolate and shortening in the microwave or stovetop double boiler over medium heat. Dip biscotti in chocolate or drizzle the chocolate on top. Sprinkle with coarse sugar.

Chai Spice Baklava

Chai tea spices lend themselves well to the rich, sweet flavor of baklava. To make it vegan, agave nectar is used in place of the honey traditionally used in baklava. This recipe is fast-paced, so have your ingredients at the ready.

YIELD: 12 TO 16 SERVINGS

FOR THE BAKLAVA:

8 OUNCES (227 G) FROZEN PHYLLO DOUGH (½ PACKAGE)

1 TEASPOON CINNAMON

¼ TEASPOON GROUND GINGER

¼ TEASPOON GROUND CARDAMOM

⅛ TEASPOON GROUND CLOVES

FRESHLY GROUND BLACK PEPPER, TO TASTE

½ CUP (112 G) VEGAN MARGARINE, MELTED

8 OUNCES (227 G) CHOPPED WALNUTS

FOR THE SYRUP:

¾ CUP PLUS 2 TABLESPOONS (206 ML) WATER

1 CHAI TEA BAG

⅔ CUP (133 G) SUGAR

¼ CUP (60 G) BROWN SUGAR

1 TEASPOON VANILLA EXTRACT

½ TEASPOON LEMON ZEST

½ CUP (120 ML) AGAVE NECTAR

To make the baklava: Preheat oven to 350°F (180°C). Line an 8-inch (20.5 cm) square baking pan with parchment paper. Remove the phyllo dough from the freezer and let thaw slightly so that it will not crack when you unroll it. Keep it under a moist towel when you start working so it doesn't dry out.

Stir the cinnamon, ginger, cardamom, cloves, and pepper into the margarine.

Layer 2 sheets of phyllo in prepared pan. Brush about one-quarter of the margarine-spice mixture and sprinkle 2 to 3 tablespoons (15 to 23 g) of chopped walnuts onto the phyllo. Repeat this process 4 more times, adding 2 more sheets of phyllo, the margarine-spice mix, and walnuts until you have 5 layers total.

Top with 6 more sheets of phyllo, brushing the margarine mix in between each layer, but no nuts. Use plain vegan margarine if you run out of the spiced margarine near the end.

Slice the baklava into squares or diamonds with a serrated knife. Place in the oven, uncovered, and bake for 40 minutes, or until the phyllo dough on top is golden.

To make the syrup: Bring the water to a boil in a small saucepan, then remove from heat.

Steep the tea bag for 10 minutes. Remove the bag, then pour in the sugars and return to medium-high heat. Bring the mixture to a boil, stirring frequently.

Stir in the vanilla, lemon zest, and agave nectar. Lower the heat and simmer the mixture for 15 to 18 minutes, stirring constantly to prevent burning.

Remove baklava from the oven, and immediately pour the syrup evenly over the surface. Let cool, then remove and set in cupcake liners for serving.

Chai Cupcakes with Vanilla Bean Buttercream

This combination of sweet and spicy transcends your average spice cake. Vanilla bean paste can be found in specialty spice or grocery stores. It imparts a true vanilla flavor and speckles without the hassle of scraping vanilla beans.

YIELD: 12 CUPCAKES

FOR THE CUPCAKES:

½ CUP (120 ML) SOY OR COCONUT CREAMER

2 BLACK TEA BAGS

½ CUP (112 G) VEGAN MARGARINE

¾ CUP (150 G) SUGAR

⅓ CUP (40 G) POWDERED SUGAR

½ CUP (115 G) VANILLA-FLAVORED NON-DAIRY YOGURT

2 TEASPOONS VANILLA EXTRACT

1½ CUPS (188 G) FLOUR

2 TEASPOONS BAKING POWDER

1½ TEASPOONS CINNAMON

¾ TEASPOON GROUND GINGER

¾ TEASPOON GROUND CARDAMOM

⅛ TEASPOON GROUND CLOVES

PINCH OF FRESHLY GRATED NUTMEG

¼ TEASPOON SALT

FOR THE TOPPING:

1½ CUPS (263 G) VEGAN CHOCOLATE CHIPS

⅓ CUP (80 ML) SOY OR COCONUT CREAMER

VANILLA BEAN BUTTERCREAM (PAGE 168)

FOR GARNISH (OPTIONAL):

CINNAMON

COARSE SUGAR

CINNAMON STICKS

VEGAN WHITE CHOCOLATE CHIPS

To make the cupcakes: Preheat oven to 350°F (180°C, or gas mark 4). Line a cupcake pan with 12 liners.

Boil the creamer and steep one of the tea bags for 10 minutes. Let cool.

Using a spice grinder or a coffee grinder, grind the contents of the other tea bag to a sand-like consistency.

Cream together margarine and sugar, then add the powdered sugar, yogurt, vanilla, infused creamer, and ground tea. Stir until combined.

Sift in flour, baking powder, spices, and salt. Distribute the batter into the prepared pan. Bake for 18 to 20 minutes, let sit in the pan for 5 minutes, then transfer to a cooling rack. Let cool completely.

To make the topping: Melt the chocolate and creamer together in the microwave or on the stovetop using a double boiler over medium heat, and stir until completely smooth.

Dip each cupcake into the ganache and place back on the cooling rack. Let ganache set.

Pipe or dollop buttercream atop cupcakes.

To garnish: Sprinkle with cinnamon and coarse sugar, and top with a cinnamon stick or a few white chocolate chips, if desired.

RECIPE NOTE

Soy or coconut creamer can be replaced with rich nondairy milk, like coconut or almond.

Earl Grey Lavender Tea Cakes

These mini cakes are infused with Earl Grey tea and fresh orange zest and topped with a lavender-infused frosting and an orange-lavender garnish. They're a perfect fit for a fancy tea party or end to a classic dinner party.

YIELD: 7 TO 8 MINI LOAF CAKES OR
10 TO 12 CUPCAKES

FOR THE LAVENDER MARGARINE:

⅓ CUP (75 G) VEGAN MARGARINE
2 TEASPOONS CULINARY LAVENDER

FOR THE CAKES:

2 EARL GREY TEA BAGS (ABOUT 1 TABLE-
   SPOON LOOSE TEA)
⅔ CUP (160 ML) NONDAIRY MILK, HEATED
⅓ CUP (80 ML) CANOLA OIL
¾ CUP (170 G) VANILLA-FLAVORED OR
   PLAIN NONDAIRY YOGURT
1 TEASPOON VANILLA EXTRACT
¾ TEASPOON ORANGE ZEST
¼ CUP (60 G) BROWN SUGAR
½ CUP (100 G) SUGAR
1⅔ CUP (208 G) FLOUR
2 TEASPOONS BAKING POWDER
¼ TEASPOON BAKING SODA
¼ TEASPOON SALT

FOR THE FROSTING:

⅓ CUP (75 G) LAVENDER MARGARINE
⅓ CUP (67 G) VEGAN SHORTENING
2 CUPS (240 G) POWDERED SUGAR
2 TEASPOONS NONDAIRY MILK

FOR THE GARNISH:

ORANGE PEEL
CULINARY LAVENDER

To make the lavender margarine: In a small saucepan, combine the margarine and lavender buds, crushing them between your fingers as you add them.

Bring to a boil over medium heat, then lower to a simmer and let cook for 20 minutes. Turn off the heat, cover, and let sit for at least 2 hours.

To make the cakes: Preheat oven to 325°F (170°C, or gas mark 3).

Grind the contents of the tea bags into a fine consistency. Dump the ground tea leaves in a large mixing bowl and pour the heated milk over them. Let steep for 5 to 10 minutes. Leave the ground tea in the batter. This will add more flavor and create speckles throughout the cakes.

Add the oil, yogurt, vanilla extract, orange zest, and sugars. Stir to combine.

Sift in the flour, baking powder, baking soda, and salt. Whisk to combine.

Fill the wells of a mini loaf pan about half full. Bake for about 25 minutes, then transfer to a wire rack to cool.

To make the frosting: Strain the lavender out of the margarine (melting if necessary) using cheesecloth or a fine metal strainer. If it's less than ⅓ cup, add plain margarine until you have ⅓ cup. Chill until solid.

Cream lavender margarine and shortening. Gradually add powdered sugar and milk and continue beating until the frosting is fluffy, 8 to 10 minutes. Pipe or spread onto cakes.

To garnish: Slice orange peels into strips with a vegetable peeler, then top with strips and lavender buds. Cheers!

RECIPE NOTE
To make cupcakes instead of tea cakes, line a cupcake pan with cupcake liners, then bake for 18 minutes in a 350°F (180°C, or gas mark 4) oven.

Arnold Palmer Loaf

Whether you call it an "Arnold Palmer" or "half and half," the 50-50 combination of black tea and lemonade lends itself perfectly to a lemon loaf with flecks of tea.

YIELD: 1 LOAF

FOR THE LOAF:

1 CUP (235 ML) NONDAIRY MILK, DIVIDED

4 BLACK TEA BAGS

1 TABLESPOON (15 ML) LEMON JUICE

1 CUP (200 G) SUGAR

¼ CUP (56 G) VEGAN MARGARINE

¼ CUP (60 ML) CANOLA OIL

1½ TABLESPOONS (9 G) LEMON ZEST

1 TEASPOON VANILLA EXTRACT

½ CUP (125 G) APPLESAUCE

2½ CUPS (312 G) FLOUR

1 TABLESPOON (14 G) BAKING POWDER

½ TEASPOON SALT

FOR THE GLAZE:

¾ CUP (90 G) POWDERED SUGAR

1 TEASPOON LEMON JUICE

2 TABLESPOONS (30 ML) BREWED BLACK TEA

To make the loaf: Preheat oven to 325°F (170°C, or gas mark 3).

Boil ¾ cup (180 ml) milk in a small saucepan, then remove from heat. Steep 3 of the tea bags in the milk for at least 10 minutes. Let cool.

Add lemon juice to the remaining ¼ cup (60 ml) milk and let sit for several minutes until it is curdled.

Cream together the sugar and margarine. Add the contents of the remaining tea bag.

Add the oil, lemon zest, vanilla extract, applesauce, and curdled milk. Stir to combine. Add the cooled black tea-milk mixture and mix until incorporated.

Sift in the flour, baking powder, and salt. Mix to combine.

Bake in an 8 x 4-inch (20.5 x 10 cm) loaf pan for about 45 minutes. After the loaf has cooled for 10 to 15 minutes, loosen the sides of the loaf from the pan with a knife, and turn it out onto the rack to continue cooling.

To make the glaze: Stir the powdered sugar into the lemon juice and tea until dissolved. Drizzle the glaze on the completely cooled loaf and let set.

RECIPE NOTE

If using loose tea instead of tea bags in the loaf, steep 1½ tablespoons tea in milk (straining after) and grind ½ tablespoon of extra tea leaves for the batter.

Thai Ice(d) Cream

Usually off-limits for vegans because of the milk or half-and-half, Thai iced tea is a cloyingly sweet, bright orange tea. The drink adapts perfectly to a coconut-based ice cream, turning this sweet beverage into a richly flavored dessert. The spice blend in this ice cream is a bit stronger than in most recipes for the drink, so it can be adjusted or scaled back to your personal tastes. Like with a good mulled wine or tea, the spices relax and meld together beautifully with time.

YIELD: 1 PINT (285 G)

1 CAN (15 OUNCES OR 440 ML) FULL-FAT COCONUT MILK

5 OR 6 CARDAMOM PODS

¼ VANILLA BEAN, SEEDS SCRAPED OUT

3 OR 4 STAR ANISE, CRUSHED

1 SMALL TAMARIND POD, SHELL AND SEEDS DISCARDED

1 CINNAMON STICK

2 WHOLE CLOVES, CRUSHED

¼ CUP (8 G) LOOSE BLACK TEA, LIGHTLY CRUSHED

1 TEASPOON DRIED ROSE PETALS

PINCH ORANGE ZEST AND/OR SQUEEZE OF LEMON JUICE

1 TEASPOON ORANGE BLOSSOM WATER

A FEW DROPS OF ORANGE FOOD COLORING (OPTIONAL)

NONDAIRY MILK (IF NEEDED)

¾ CUP (150 G) SUGAR

Combine the coconut milk and the cardamom, vanilla bean, star anise, tamarind, cinnamon stick, and cloves in a small saucepan over medium-high heat. Bring to a boil, then reduce the heat and let simmer for 5 to 6 minutes.

Turn off the heat, then add the tea, rose petals, orange and/or lemon, orange blossom water, food coloring (if using), and sugar, stirring to dissolve. Let sit for 15 minutes.

Strain the spices and tea out of the mixture into a liquid measuring cup. Add some nondairy milk if the mixture is too thick to strain. The mixture should equal 2 cups (470 ml). Transfer the mixture to a sealed container and refrigerate for 5 to 6 hours, or overnight.

Freeze in an ice cream maker according to manufacturer's instructions. Serve in a glass garnished with whole spices and perhaps a bit of coconut milk poured on top.

RECIPE NOTE
Thai tea gets its orange color from the tea concentrate commonly used, but since we're steeping black tea and whole spices, the color will be muted. If desired, add a few drops of orange food coloring to brighten the color.

Agua de Jamaica Key Lime Pie

This brightly colored key lime pie is drizzled with a sweet and tangy hibiscus syrup. The name comes from hibiscus tea, also called *agua de Jamaica*, a sweet iced tea made with hibiscus flowers and lime. You can find dried hibiscus flowers at tea shops, spice stores, and grocery stores with large bulk spice sections. And if you don't have time to make a crust, feel free to use a store-bought one (just check the ingredients first).

YIELD: 12 SERVINGS

FOR THE CRUST:

1½ CUPS (180 G) GRAHAM CRACKER CRUMBS
¼ CUP (56 G) VEGAN MARGARINE, MELTED
¼ CUP (50 G) SUGAR

FOR THE FILLING:

1⅔ CUPS (395 ML) NONDAIRY MILK
½ CUP (120 ML) LIME JUICE (ABOUT 4 MEDIUM LIMES, OR 5 TO 6 IF USING SMALLER KEY LIMES)
1 TABLESPOON (6 G) LIME ZEST
⅓ CUP (43 G) CORNSTARCH OR ARROW-ROOT POWDER
¾ CUP (150 G) SUGAR
4 OUNCES (114 G) VEGAN CREAM CHEESE (½ TUB)

FOR THE SYRUP:

1 CUP (235 ML) WATER
¼ CUP (66 G) DRIED HIBISCUS FLOWERS
½ CUP (100 G) SUGAR

To make the crust: Preheat oven to 375°F (190°C, or gas mark 5).

Combine all ingredients in a mixing bowl and stir thoroughly. If the crumbs are dry or won't hold together when pressed, add a splash of nondairy milk to the bowl.

Grease a standard 9-inch (23 cm) pie plate with margarine or cooking spray, then press the graham cracker mixture evenly over the bottom and up the sides. Bake for 8 to 10 minutes, or until firm. Set aside to cool.

To make the filling: Combine all filling ingredients except the cream cheese in a medium saucepan and whisk to dissolve corn-starch. Turn the heat up to medium and stir frequently with whisk until very thick, 8 to 9 minutes.

Turn off heat, then stir in the cream cheese until smooth.

Let sit for 2 to 3 minutes until slightly cooled, then pour into prepared graham cracker crust. Cool completely on cooling rack, then cover and transfer to the refrigerator until firm.

To make the syrup: Combine the water and hibiscus in a small saucepan and bring to a boil over medium heat. Boil for 8 minutes.

Turn off the heat, then strain out flowers with a slotted spoon. Add the sugar, then turn the heat back on and stir until the mixture becomes syrupy, 6 to 8 minutes. Remove from heat and let cool. The syrup will thicken as it cools.

To serve: Drizzle a slice of pie with hibiscus syrup, and garnish with lime slices and hibiscus flowers.

> **RECIPE NOTE**
> Be careful while making the syrup, as hibiscus will stain towels and some surfaces. Don't use cookware or utensils that stain easily.

CHAPTER 4

the lemonade stand

Summery, citrus flavors and sugary drinks found at lemonade stands blend perfectly with cupcakes, sponge cakes, and sugar cookies. Lemonade was meant to be a cupcake!

Grape Juice Pudding

This recipe is based on Swedish grape juice pudding with the addition of candied lemon zest and toasted almonds. The candied lemon zest can be made ahead of time.

YIELD: 4 SERVINGS

FOR THE PUDDING:
2 CUPS (470 ML) GRAPE JUICE
¼ CUP (32 G) CORNSTARCH
¼ CUP (50 G) SUGAR
¼ TEASPOON SALT
1 TABLESPOON (15 ML) LEMON JUICE

FOR THE GARNISH:
2 CUPS (470 ML) WATER
2 LEMONS
1 CUP (200 G) SUGAR
¼ CUP (28 G) SLICED ALMONDS
VEGAN WHIPPED CREAM (OPTIONAL)

To make the pudding: Whisk together ½ cup (120 ml) of the grape juice with the cornstarch in a medium saucepan with the stove off. Turn the heat to medium and pour in the rest of the grape juice, stirring constantly.

Add the sugar and salt and stir until dissolved. Continue stirring frequently until the pudding thickens, about 8 minutes. Add the lemon juice at the 5-minute mark.

Pour into ½-cup (120 ml) pudding or ice cream dishes. Let cool, then cover and chill in the fridge until ready to serve.

To make the garnish: Bring 1 cup of the water to a simmer. Peel the zest off the lemons in long strips with a vegetable peeler, then slice the strips into thinner ribbons. Let the lemon zest simmer for 6 minutes, then drain out the water. Keep the lemon zest in the saucepan.

Pour the other cup of water into the saucepan, along with ¾ cup (150 g) sugar. Pour the other ¼ cup (50 g) sugar on a plate or in a shallow bowl. Set aside. Bring to a simmer over low heat until the lemon zest is translucent and the syrup is a bit thick, 10 to 15 minutes. Turn off the heat and remove the lemon zest from the pot with a slotted spoon. Let the syrup drip off, then roll the zest on the plate of sugar to coat.

Spread the candied zest on a parchment-lined cookie sheet and let dry uncovered for several hours or overnight.

Preheat oven to 350°F (180°C, or gas mark 4). Spread the sliced almonds on a cookie sheet and bake until golden and fragrant, 3 to 5 minutes.

To serve, sprinkle lemon zest and toasted almonds atop each cup of pudding. Add vegan whipped cream if desired.

Lavender Lemonade Cupcakes

These cupcakes take a bit of preparation, but in the end you will be dazzled with a fluffy lemon cupcake topped with a lavender-infused lemon frosting that is perfect for summer.

YIELD: 12 CUPCAKES

FOR THE LAVENDER MARGARINE:
½ CUP (112 G) VEGAN MARGARINE
1 TABLESPOON (8 G) CULINARY
    LAVENDER

FOR THE CUPCAKES:
½ CUP (112 G) VEGAN MARGARINE
⅔ CUP (133 G) SUGAR
⅓ CUP (40 G) POWDERED SUGAR
½ CUP (115 G) NONDAIRY YOGURT
⅓ CUP (80 ML) NONDAIRY MILK
1 TABLESPOON (6 G) LEMON ZEST
1 TABLESPOON (15 ML) LEMON JUICE
1 TEASPOON VANILLA EXTRACT
1½ CUPS (188 G) FLOUR
2 TEASPOONS BAKING POWDER
¼ TEASPOON SALT

FOR THE FROSTING:
½ CUP (100 G) VEGAN SHORTENING
2¾ CUPS (330 G) POWDERED SUGAR
1 TABLESPOON (15 ML) LEMON JUICE
½ TEASPOON LEMON ZEST

To make the lavender margarine: In a small saucepan, combine the margarine and lavender buds, crushing them between your fingers as you add them.

Bring to a boil over medium heat, then lower to a simmer and let cook for 20 minutes. Turn off the heat, cover, and let sit for at least 2 hours.

To make the cupcakes: Preheat oven to 350°F (180°C, or gas mark 4) and line a cupcake pan with 12 liners.

Cream together margarine and sugars until smooth. Add yogurt, milk, lemon zest and juice, and vanilla extract. Continue mixing until everything is combined.

Sift in flour, baking powder, and salt and whisk until just combined. The batter should be somewhat thick and fragrant.

Using an ice cream scoop or large spoon, distribute the batter, filling each cupcake liner a little over half full. Bake for 18 minutes or until the tops are firm and a toothpick inserted in the center comes out clean.

Transfer to a wire rack to cool.

To make the frosting: Using cheesecloth or a fine metal strainer, strain the lavender out of the margarine (melting if necessary).

If it measures less than ½ cup (113 g), make up the difference by adding some plain margarine. Chill until solid.

Cream together lavender margarine and vegan shortening. Gradually add powdered sugar.

When almost all the sugar is incorporated, add the lemon juice and lemon zest. Continue beating until completely smooth and fluffy, 8 to 10 minutes.

Spoon frosting into a pastry bag and pipe swirls atop your cupcakes. Garnish with a fresh lemon slice and a sprinkle of lavender buds.

Rosewater Lemonade Cupcakes

This cupcake would be the perfect ending after a falafel sandwich. It's inspired by the icy cold rosewater-infused lemonade at Middle Eastern restaurants.

YIELD: 12 CUPCAKES

FOR THE CUPCAKES:

½ CUP (112 G) VEGAN MARGARINE
⅔ CUP (133 G) SUGAR
⅓ CUP (40 G) POWDERED SUGAR
½ CUP (115 G) NONDAIRY YOGURT
⅓ CUP (80 ML) NONDAIRY MILK
1 TABLESPOON (6 G) LEMON ZEST
1 TABLESPOON (15 ML) LEMON JUICE
1 TEASPOON VANILLA EXTRACT
2 TEASPOONS ROSEWATER
1½ CUPS (188 G) FLOUR
2 TEASPOONS BAKING POWDER
¼ TEASPOON SALT

FOR THE FROSTING:

½ CUP (112 G) VEGAN MARGARINE
½ CUP (100 G) VEGAN SHORTENING
3 CUPS (360 G) POWDERED SUGAR
2 TEASPOONS LEMON JUICE
2 TO 3 TEASPOONS ROSEWATER
¼ TEASPOON LEMON ZEST

To make the cupcakes: Preheat oven to 350°F (180°C, or gas mark 4) and line a cupcake pan with 12 liners.

Cream together the margarine and sugars until smooth, then add yogurt, milk, lemon zest and juice, vanilla extract, and rosewater. Continue mixing until everything is combined.

Sift in flour, baking powder, and salt and whisk until just combined. The batter should be somewhat thick and fragrant.

Using an ice cream scoop or large spoon, distribute the batter, filling each cupcake liner a little over half full.

Bake for 18 minutes or until the tops are firm and a toothpick inserted in the center comes out clean. Transfer to a wire rack to cool.

To make the frosting: Cream together margarine and shortening. Gradually add powdered sugar. When almost all the sugar is incorporated, add the lemon juice, rosewater, and lemon zest. Continue beating until completely smooth and fluffy, 8 to 10 minutes.

Spoon frosting into a pastry bag and pipe swirls atop your cupcakes. Garnish with lemon slices and rose petals.

Strawberry Balsamic Crush Cupcakes

Strawberry crush is an icy, refreshing drink that involves muddling strawberries with fruit, herbs, and tangy balsamic. This strawberry balsamic chocolate cake is filled with basil-infused cream, engulfed with a balsamic chocolate coating, and garnished with a strawberry and basil leaf.

YIELD: 12 CUPCAKES

FOR THE CUPCAKES:

1 TABLESPOON (15 ML) BALSAMIC VINEGAR

⅓ CUP (56 G) CHOPPED STRAWBERRIES

1⅓ CUPS (167 G) FLOUR

⅓ CUP (40 G) COCOA POWDER

¾ CUP (150 G) SUGAR

1 TEASPOON BAKING SODA

¼ TEASPOON SALT

⅓ CUP (80 ML) CANOLA OIL

¾ CUP (176 ML) NONDAIRY MILK

¼ CUP (80 G) STRAWBERRY JAM

½ TEASPOON VANILLA EXTRACT

3 TABLESPOONS (45 ML) BALSAMIC VINEGAR

1 TABLESPOON (2.5 G) FRESH BASIL, CHOPPED

1 TABLESPOON (15 ML) BASIL SIMPLE
   SYRUP (PAGE 168)

FOR THE FROSTING:

¼ CUP (56 G) VEGAN MARGARINE

¼ CUP (50 G) VEGAN SHORTENING

2 CUPS (240 G) POWDERED SUGAR

2 TO 3 TABLESPOONS (30 TO 45 ML) BASIL
   SIMPLE SYRUP, PLUS MORE AS NEEDED

1 TABLESPOON (2.5 G) FRESH BASIL, CHOPPED

FOR THE GANACHE:

¾ CUP (131 G) VEGAN CHOCOLATE CHIPS

¼ CUP (60 ML) NONDAIRY MILK

2 TABLESPOONS (30 ML) BALSAMIC VINEGAR

FOR THE GARNISH:

STRAWBERRIES

FRESH BASIL LEAVES

To make the cupcakes: Preheat oven to 350°F (180°C, or gas mark 4). Fill a cupcake pan with 12 liners. Stir the balsamic vinegar into the chopped strawberries and let sit for 15 to 20 minutes.

Combine flour, cocoa powder, sugar, baking soda, and salt in a stand mixer or mixing bowl.

Create a well in the center of the dry ingredients and add canola oil, milk, strawberry jam, vanilla extract, balsamic vinegar, chopped basil, Basil Simple Syrup, and strawberry-balsamic mixture. Mix until just combined.

Using an ice cream scoop or large spoon, fill each cupcake liner a little more than halfway. Bake for 18 to 20 minutes, until the tops of the cupcakes are firm and a toothpick inserted in the center comes out clean. Transfer to a wire rack to cool.

To make the frosting: Cream together margarine and shortening. Gradually add the powdered sugar. Drizzle in the syrup as you add powdered sugar. Using a hand or stand mixer, beat the frosting for 6 to 8 minutes. Add basil leaves and continue mixing until fluffy.

To fill cooled cupcakes with frosting: Fill a pastry bag (or plastic zip-top bag with the corner cut) with frosting. Using your pinky finger or the end of a spoon, poke a hole in the center of each cupcake and squeeze in the frosting. Repeat for each cupcake.

To make the ganache: Melt chocolate chips with the milk in a glass bowl in the microwave or on the stove in a double boiler over medium heat. Remove from heat and stir in the balsamic vinegar, completely incorporating it into the chocolate.

Dip cupcake tops in the ganache, letting any excess drip off. Return the cupcakes to the cooling rack.

To garnish: Top each cupcake with a strawberry and a basil leaf.

Mango Lassi Cake

The most appropriate form for a mango lassi, besides the actual drink, is a light and fluffy delicately flavored cake. It's perfect to finish a meal of samosas and curry.

YIELD: 9 TO 12 SERVINGS

FOR THE CAKE:

½ CUP (120 ML) CANOLA OIL

1 CUP (200 G) SUGAR

6 OUNCES (170 G) PLAIN OR VANILLA-
FLAVORED NONDAIRY YOGURT

1 TEASPOON VANILLA EXTRACT

¼ TEASPOON COCONUT EXTRACT

½ CUP (120 ML) ALMOND MILK

2 CUPS (250 G) FLOUR

2 TEASPOONS BAKING POWDER

½ TEASPOON BAKING SODA

¼ TEASPOON SALT

1 RIPE MANGO

FOR THE YOGURT GLAZE:

⅓ CUP (77 G) MANGO- OR VANILLA-
FLAVORED NONDAIRY YOGURT

½ CUP (60 ML) POWDERED SUGAR

FOR GARNISH:

1 RIPE MANGO, SLICED

To make the cake: Preheat oven to 325°F (170°C, or gas mark 3). Line the bottom and sides of an 8-inch (20.5 cm) square pan with parchment paper.

In a large bowl, mix together the oil, sugar, yogurt, extracts, and milk, then stir to combine.

Sift in the flour, baking powder, baking soda, and salt, then whisk until smooth. Peel and chop the mango into ½-inch (1 cm) pieces and stir into the batter, which should be thick.

Pour batter into the pan and bake for 30 to 35 minutes or until the center is firm and doesn't look wet. Transfer to a wire rack to cool.

To make the yogurt glaze: Stir the yogurt and powdered sugar together and set aside. When the cake is cooled, slice into 9 to 12 squares. Drizzle each piece with about 1 tablespoon (15 ml) of the yogurt glaze and top with a mango slice. Serve!

Grape Kool-Aid Whoopie Pies

Two airy, pillowy cakes with a burst of grape flavor are sandwiched around a sweet and fluffy buttercream filling. The grape flavor is courtesy of a packet of Kool-Aid mixed into the batter. Perfect for a kid's party or summer treat, they're guaranteed to make anyone bounce off the walls with a sugar high.

YIELD: 9 OR 10 WHOOPIE PIES

FOR THE PIES:
¼ CUP (50 G) VEGAN SHORTENING
¼ CUP (56 G) VEGAN MARGARINE
¾ CUP (150 G) SUGAR
1 PACKAGE GRAPE KOOL-AID (OR ALTERNATIVE 0.14-OUNCE POWDERED DRINK MIX)
⅓ CUP (40 G) POWDERED SUGAR
⅓ CUP (82 G) APPLESAUCE
½ CUP (120 ML) NONDAIRY MILK
1 TEASPOON VANILLA EXTRACT
2¼ CUPS (281 G) FLOUR
2 TEASPOONS BAKING POWDER
½ TEASPOON BAKING SODA
¼ TEASPOON SALT

FOR THE FROSTING:
⅓ CUP (67 G) VEGAN SHORTENING
⅓ CUP (75 G) VEGAN MARGARINE
2¼ CUPS (270 G) POWDERED SUGAR
1 TO 2 TABLESPOONS (15 TO 30 ML) NONDAIRY MILK
PURPLE FOOD COLORING

To make the pies: Preheat oven to 375°F (190°C, or gas mark 5).

Cream together shortening and margarine in a stand mixer or by hand. Add the sugar and Kool-Aid and continue mixing until thoroughly combined and fluffy.

Pour in powdered sugar and applesauce and continue beating. Add milk and vanilla and mix until completely incorporated.

Sift in flour, baking powder and baking soda, and salt. Beat until all the flour is thoroughly mixed into the wet ingredients. The dough should be thick, lightweight, and fluffy. Refrigerate the dough for 15 to 20 minutes.

Using an ice cream scoop or a large spoon, drop 3-tablespoon (about 45 g) portions of dough onto a cookie sheet lined with parchment paper, enough for 18 to 20 whoopie pie halves. Do not flatten. Bake for 12 to 14 minutes or until the tops are firm and the edges start to turn golden. Let cool.

To make the frosting: Cream together the shortening and margarine, then gradually add the powdered sugar while you mix. Add milk and food coloring, a few drops at a time, until you reach your desired color. Whip until fluffy, 6 to 8 minutes.

Spread a thick layer of frosting on one half of a whoopie pie, and sandwich it together with another half. Repeat for all the whoopie pies.

Store in an airtight container, separated from one another, for up to 2 weeks. Like cupcakes, these whoopie pies have a tendency to stick together and rip apart if stored on top of each other.

Strawberry Kool-Aid Cookies

Neon pink and intensely strawberry-flavored, these cookies are quite different, but strangely addictive. The strawberry Kool-Aid can be replaced with any other flavor, or multiple flavors can be used for a rainbow of cookies.

YIELD: 18 TO 20 COOKIES

½ CUP (120 ML) NONDAIRY MILK
2 TEASPOONS APPLE CIDER VINEGAR
⅓ CUP (80 ML) CANOLA OIL
½ CUP (100 G) SUGAR
½ CUP (115 G) BROWN SUGAR
1 TABLESPOON (8 G) CORNSTARCH
1 PACKAGE STRAWBERRY KOOL-AID
    (OR ALTERNATIVE 0.14-OUNCE
    POWDERED DRINK MIX)
1 TEASPOON VANILLA EXTRACT
2¼ CUPS (281 G) FLOUR
1½ TEASPOONS BAKING SODA
½ TEASPOON BAKING POWDER
¼ TEASPOON SALT

Preheat oven to 350°F (180°C, or gas mark 4).

Combine the milk and apple cider vinegar in a mixing bowl or stand mixer and let sit for 2 to 3 minutes, until it curdles.

Add the canola oil, sugars, cornstarch, Kool-Aid, and vanilla to the bowl and stir until combined.

Sift in the flour, baking soda, baking powder, and salt. Mix until completely combined. The dough should be thick and somewhat sticky.

Drop heaping tablespoons of dough onto a parchment-lined cookie sheet and flatten slightly.

Bake for 12 to 14 minutes, or until the tops are firm and the edges are starting to turn golden.

Let cool on the tray for 5 minutes, then transfer to a wire rack to cool. Let cool completely before eating.

Carrot Juice Oatmeal Cream Pies

These pies taste like carrot cake. Forgo the filling entirely for some amazing carrot oatmeal cookies. Adding raisins or nuts to the cookies is a tasty variation.

FOR THE COOKIES:

⅓ CUP (80 ML) CANOLA OIL

⅔ CUP (150 G) BROWN SUGAR

½ CUP (100 G) SUGAR

2 TEASPOONS MOLASSES

1 TEASPOON VANILLA EXTRACT

¾ CUP (82.5 G) GRATED CARROTS

¼ CUP (60 ML) CARROT JUICE

2 CUPS (250 G) FLOUR

1¼ CUPS (100 G) QUICK-COOKING OATS

1 TEASPOON BAKING SODA

¾ TEASPOON CINNAMON

½ TEASPOON GROUND GINGER

⅛ TEASPOON FRESHLY GRATED NUTMEG

⅛ TEASPOON GROUND CLOVES

¼ TEASPOON SALT

FOR THE PINEAPPLE BUTTERCREAM:

2 TABLESPOONS (25 G) VEGAN
   SHORTENING

2 TABLESPOONS (28 G) VEGAN MARGARINE

1¼ CUPS (150 G) POWDERED SUGAR

¼ TEASPOON CINNAMON

½ TEASPOON VANILLA EXTRACT

3 TABLESPOONS (30 G) FINELY CHOPPED
   FRESH OR CANNED PINEAPPLE

To make the cookies: Preheat oven to 350°F (180°C, or gas mark 4).

Stir together the oil, sugars, molasses, vanilla, grated carrots, and carrot juice in a mixing bowl.

Add flour, oats, baking soda, spices, and salt and mix until just combined. The texture should be thick, like oatmeal cookie dough. Adjust the texture with additional carrot juice or flour, if necessary.

Place golf ball–sized portions of dough on a parchment-lined cookie sheet. Flatten slightly and bake for 9 to 10 minutes, until the tops are firm and the edges look golden and crispy. Let cool on the cookie sheet for 3 to 4 minutes, then transfer to a wire rack to cool completely.

To make the pineapple buttercream: Mix together the shortening and margarine with a fork in a small mixing bowl.

Gradually add the powdered sugar, mixing after each inclusion until the whole cup is added. Stir in the cinnamon, vanilla extract, and pineapple.

If the buttercream is too sticky or watery, add additional powdered sugar. If it's too thick, drizzle in some pineapple juice until it reaches a fluffy consistency.

Spread a dollop of cream on the inside of one cookie, then top with another cookie. Repeat for all cream pies.

Cherry Bourbon Fried Pies

Fried pies and bourbon, two iconic Southern indulgences, join together for a delicious summer treat.

FOR THE FILLING:

1½ CUPS (233 G) FRESH CHERRIES, PITTED AND HALVED

1 TABLESPOON (8 G) CORNSTARCH

⅓ CUP (67 G) SUGAR

2 TABLESPOONS (30 ML) BOURBON

FOR THE CRUST

3 CUPS (375 G) FLOUR

1 TEASPOON BAKING POWDER

½ TEASPOON SALT

3 TABLESPOONS (39 G) SUGAR

½ CUP (100 G) VEGAN SHORTENING OR COCONUT OIL

½ CUP (120 ML) COLD WATER PLUS 1 TEASPOON (5 ML) APPLE CIDER VINEGAR

¼ CUP (60 ML) VODKA

VEGETABLE OIL, FOR FRYING

POWDERED SUGAR, FOR DUSTING

To make the filling: Combine the cherries, cornstarch, and sugar into a small saucepan over medium heat. Stir vigorously until the cornstarch dissolves.

Cook for 5 to 6 minutes, stirring frequently until the sugar dissolves and creates a syrup consistency. Remove from heat and stir in the bourbon.

To make the crust: Place the flour, baking powder, salt, and sugar into a large bowl and cut in the shortening until the dough resembles pebbles. Stir in the water-vinegar mixture and vodka and mix until completely incorporated and the dough is of rolling consistency.

Take golf ball–sized pieces of pastry and roll them out into 5-inch (12.5 cm) circles. Place 1 tablespoon (15 ml) fruit filling on one half of the circle.

Wet the edges of each circle, then fold it over into a half-moon shape. Seal the edges by crimping them with a fork. Repeat for each pie. Place prepared pies on a baking sheet and chill in the refrigerator for 30 minutes.

Fill a large pot or Dutch oven with at least 2 inches (5 cm) of vegetable oil and heat to around 350°F (180°C) over medium heat (or when a piece of dough tossed into the oil rises to the top and bubbles).

Fry 3 or 4 pies at a time until they turn golden, flipping halfway through, 2 to 3 minutes on each side.

Place fried pies on a wire rack with a cookie sheet underneath that is covered with paper towels or brown paper bags to catch oil drips. Dust with powdered sugar before serving.

REPLACING THE ALCOHOL
Vodka makes a tender, flaky crust, but it can be replaced with cold water. Omit the bourbon from the filling.

RECIPE NOTES
- To make Strawberry Daiquiri Pies, replace the cherries with strawberries, the bourbon with rum, and add 1 teaspoon (2 g) lime zest to the filling.
- You can also replace the cherries with another fruit, like apples, peaches, or apricot for fun variations.

Tropical Smoothie Pudding

Pudding is not often laced with either pizzazz or flavor variations, so this tropical pudding is dressed up like a cocktail.

YIELD: 4 OR 5 SERVINGS (½ CUP
[115 G] EACH)

FOR THE PUDDING:

1 CAN (15 OUNCES OR 440 ML) FULL-FAT
   COCONUT MILK

¼ CUP (32 G) CORNSTARCH

½ CUP (115 G) BROWN SUGAR

1 CUP (235 ML) COCONUT MILK
   (FROM A CARTON, NOT A CAN)

⅓ CUP (52 G) CHOPPED FRESH OR
   CANNED PINEAPPLE

1 BANANA, MASHED

½ CUP (78 G) FINELY CHOPPED
   CHERRIES

¼ CUP (60 ML) ORANGE JUICE

1 TEASPOON VANILLA EXTRACT

FOR GARNISH:

STRAWBERRIES

ORANGE SLICES

BANANA SLICES

CHERRIES

SHREDDED COCONUT

COCKTAIL UMBRELLAS

To make pudding: Combine the can of coconut milk with the cornstarch in a medium saucepan and whisk together with the heat off until the cornstarch is dissolved.

Turn on the stove to medium heat. While you continue to whisk constantly, add the brown sugar and gradually pour in the coconut milk from the carton.

Whisk for 5 to 10 minutes, or until the pudding thickens. Stir in the pineapple, banana, cherries, and orange juice. Continue stirring for a minute or two more, until the pudding is completely thickened. Remove from heat and stir in the vanilla.

Pour the pudding into individual cups and let chill for an hour or more. Garnish with fruit slices, shredded coconut, and a cocktail umbrella and serve!

RECIPE NOTE

The cherries can be replaced with strawberries or another brightly colored fruit. Otherwise, the pudding may turn an off-putting shade of gray from the banana. If you want additional color, add some beet juice or natural food coloring.

Watermelon Fresca Sorbet

The key to making an alluring sorbet is texture and fresh, natural flavors so that it stands on its own, rather than in comparison to ice cream or gelato. This is watermelon fresca in sorbet form, employing fresh watermelon, limes, and homemade mint syrup. Any leftover syrup can be used in mojitos, *agua fresca*, or lemonade.

YIELD: 1 QUART (940 ML)

6 CUPS (900 G) CUBED WATERMELON
¾ CUP (176 ML) MINT SIMPLE SYRUP
  (PAGE 168)
3 TABLESPOONS (45 ML) LIME JUICE

Combine all ingredients in a blender or food processor and blend until smooth. Freeze in an ice cream maker according to manufacturer's instructions. Serve garnished with mint leaves and lime wedges.

RECIPE NOTE
For a variation, add ½ cup (78 g) fresh cherries to the blender for an extra burst of flavor and a deeper red color.

Basil Agave Lemonade Pops

These popsicles are made to appeal to the over-five-years-old crowd, infusing lemonade with fresh basil and the delicate flavor of agave nectar.

YIELD: 4 POPS, DEPENDING ON THE
SIZE OF YOUR MOLDS

¼ CUP (10 G) FRESH BASIL LEAVES
¼ CUP (60 ML) AGAVE NECTAR
3 TABLESPOONS (45 ML) WATER
½ CUP (120 ML) LEMON JUICE
½ CUP (120 ML) WATER

Stack the basil leaves atop each other, roll the stack up tightly, then slice the roll of basil finely to produce thin ribbons. This is called chiffonade and will allow the basil to infuse the syrup with the most flavor.

Combine the agave nectar and 3 tablespoons (45 ml) water in a saucepan over medium-high heat and stir until combined. Bring to a boil, and let boil for 1 minute, stirring constantly.

Remove from heat and stir in the basil. Completely submerge the leaves and coat thoroughly with the agave nectar. Basil loses its flavor at high temperatures, so don't be tempted to put the saucepan back on the heat. Let the basil sit in the agave nectar for 45 minutes to 1 hour, uncovered.

Once cool, strain out the basil and stir in the lemon juice and ½ cup (120 ml) water. Pour into ice pop molds or small cups with popsicle sticks, then freeze until solid.

RECIPE NOTE
Toss a few fresh blueberries or raspberries in each ice pop right before freezing.

the soda fountain

Diner-style favorites! Enjoy your root beer float three ways: whoopie pies, ice cream sandwiches, and cupcakes. Shirley Temples! Chocolate malt shakes! It's the bee's knees!

Shirley Temple Cookies

These cookies are meant to replicate Shirley Temple drinks. Not the sad, fake corn syrup–flavored concoction, but real kiddie cocktails—fizzy citrus-cherry flavored drinks topped with fruit slices, umbrellas, and cherries on cocktail swords to make every eight-year-old at weddings and social functions feel grown up and sophisticated.

YIELD: 24 COOKIES

FOR THE COOKIES:

½ CUP (112 G) VEGAN MARGARINE

¼ CUP (60 ML) CANOLA OIL

1 CUP (120 G) POWDERED SUGAR

1½ TEASPOONS LEMON ZEST

1½ TEASPOONS ORANGE ZEST

1 TABLESPOON (15 ML) LEMON JUICE

1 TABLESPOON (15 ML) ORANGE JUICE

¼ TEASPOON ALMOND EXTRACT

2 CUPS (250 G) FLOUR

¼ TEASPOON BAKING POWDER

¼ TEASPOON BAKING SODA

¼ TEASPOON SALT

GRANULATED SUGAR, FOR SPRINKLING

FOR THE TOPPINGS:

CHERRY BUTTERCREAM (PAGE 168)

MARASCHINO CHERRIES

SOUR OR FIZZY CANDIES

To make the cookies: Preheat oven to 350°F (180°C, or gas mark 4).

Stir together the margarine and oil in a large mixing bowl. Gradually add the powdered sugar, then stir in the zests, juices, and almond extract.

Sift in the flour, baking powder, baking soda, and salt and mix until just combined. The dough should be somewhat thick.

Drop dough by the tablespoon onto a parchment-lined cookie sheet and sprinkle a pinch of granulated sugar over each cookie. Bake for 10 to 12 minutes, until the bottoms are golden and the cookies are firm. The flavors are delicate, so be careful not to over-bake them. Transfer to a wire rack to cool.

To garnish: Spread or pipe the cherry buttercream frosting onto the cookies. Top each cookie with a cherry half and candy, then serve!

Coconut Shirley Temple Cupcakes

Inspired by the Shirley Temple Cookies on the previous page, these cupcakes are funky and flavorful, with a tropical twist. Have fun with the decorations to make them adorable!

YIELD: 12 CUPCAKES

FOR THE CUPCAKES:

1 TEASPOON LEMON JUICE

⅔ CUP (160 ML) COCONUT MILK

½ CUP (112 G) VEGAN MARGARINE

⅔ CUP (133 G) SUGAR

½ CUP (60 G) POWDERED SUGAR

2½ TEASPOONS LEMON ZEST

1 TEASPOON ORANGE ZEST

1 TABLESPOON (15 ML) LEMON JUICE

1 TABLESPOON (15 ML) ORANGE JUICE

1 TEASPOON VANILLA EXTRACT

1½ CUPS (188 G) FLOUR

2 TEASPOONS BAKING POWDER

¼ TEASPOON SALT

FOR THE TOPPINGS:

CHERRY BUTTERCREAM (PAGE 168)

COCKTAIL UMBRELLAS

MARASCHINO CHERRIES

COLORED SUGAR AND SPRINKLES

SOUR OR FIZZY CANDIES

To make the cupcakes: Preheat oven to 350°F (180°C, or gas mark 4) and line a cupcake pan with 12 liners.

Squeeze the lemon juice into the coconut milk and let sit for 5 minutes to curdle. Cream together the margarine and sugars until smooth, then add the coconut milk–lemon juice mixture, lemon and orange zests and juices, and vanilla extract. Continue mixing until everything is combined.

Sift in the flour, baking powder, and salt and whisk until just combined. The batter should be somewhat thick and fragrant.

Using an ice cream scoop or large spoon, fill each cupcake liner a little over half full. Bake for 18 minutes or until the tops are firm and a toothpick inserted in the center comes out clean. Transfer to a wire rack to cool.

To garnish: Spoon frosting into a pastry bag and pipe swirls atop your cupcakes. Garnish with a paper umbrella, maraschino cherry, sprinkles, and candies.

Grape Soda Cupcakes

These cupcakes and the frosting are infused with grape soda. Although they appear to be suited to just a child's palate, grown-ups will be pleasantly surprised.

YIELD: 12 CUPCAKES

FOR THE CUPCAKES:

5 CUPS (940 ML) GRAPE SODA, DIVIDED

1½ CUPS (188 G) FLOUR

3 TABLESPOONS (22 G) COCOA POWDER

¾ CUP (150 G) SUGAR

1 TEASPOON BAKING SODA

¼ TEASPOON SALT

⅓ CUP (80 ML) CANOLA OIL

½ TEASPOON VANILLA EXTRACT

1 TEASPOON APPLE CIDER VINEGAR

FOR THE FROSTING:

⅓ CUP (67 G) VEGAN SHORTENING

⅓ CUP (75 G) VEGAN MARGARINE

2¼ CUPS (270 G) POWDERED SUGAR

To make the cupcakes: Pour 4 cups (940 ml) of the grape soda into a saucepan and bring to a boil over medium-high heat. Reduce to a low boil and let boil for 30 minutes, reducing the soda to ¾ cup (176 ml). If you reduce it too much, simply reconstitute it to make ¾ cup (176 ml). Set aside.

Preheat oven to 350°F (180°C, or gas mark 4). Combine the flour, cocoa powder, sugar, baking soda, and salt in a stand mixer or mixing bowl. Stir until combined.

Create a well in the center of the dry ingredients and add the canola oil, the remaining 1 cup of grape soda, ¼ cup (60 ml) grape soda reduction, vanilla extract, and apple cider vinegar. Mix until just combined.

Using a cupcake scoop, fill each cupcake liner a little more than halfway. Bake for 16 to 18 minutes, until the tops of the cupcakes are firm and a toothpick inserted into the center comes out clean. Transfer to a wire rack to cool.

To make the frosting: Cream together margarine and shortening. Gradually add the powdered sugar, sifting as you go. Once half the powdered sugar is mixed in, start drizzling in 3 tablespoons (45 g) of the grape soda reduction.

Mix until completely incorporated and beat the frosting for 6 to 8 minutes using a hand or stand mixer. Add more powdered sugar or grape soda reduction to adjust the consistency of the frosting if necessary.

Dip the tops of the cupcakes in grape soda reduction, then pipe or spoon on some frosting. Drizzle with ½ teaspoon grape soda reduction. Repeat for all cupcakes. Top with sprinkles or other colorful candies and edible glitter. Serve!

RECIPE NOTE
The grape soda reduction is needed in the cupcake batter, frosting, dip, and drizzle, so remember to save some as you go.

Banana Butterscotch Shake Cupcakes

The tropical fruit takes center stage in a fluffy cupcake amped up with butterscotch flavor, miles away from banana nut muffins.

YIELD: 12 CUPCAKES

½ CUP (112 G) VEGAN MARGARINE
¾ CUP (150 G) SUGAR
⅓ CUP (40 G) POWDERED SUGAR
¾ CUP (170 G) MASHED BANANA
½ CUP (120 ML) NONDAIRY MILK
¼ TEASPOON BUTTERSCOTCH EXTRACT
2 TEASPOONS VANILLA EXTRACT
1½ CUPS (188 G) FLOUR
2 TEASPOONS BAKING POWDER
¼ TEASPOON SALT
BUTTERSCOTCH BUTTERCREAM
   (PAGE 168)

Preheat oven to 350°F (180°C, or gas mark 4) and line a cupcake pan with 12 liners.

Cream together the margarine and sugar until smooth, then add the powdered sugar, banana, milk, and butterscotch and vanilla extracts. Continue mixing until everything is combined.

Sift in the flour, baking powder, and salt and whisk until just combined. The batter should be somewhat thick.

Using an ice cream scoop or large spoon, fill each cupcake liner a little over half full. Bake for 18 minutes or until the tops are firm and a toothpick inserted in the center comes out clean. Transfer to a wire rack to cool.

Spoon Butterscotch Buttercream frosting into a pastry bag and pipe swirls atop your cupcakes.

Hot Chocolate Marshmallow Mousse Brownies

These brownies are dense and fudgy, topped with rich chocolate mousse and mini marshmallows.

YIELD: 9 TO 12 BROWNIES

FOR THE BROWNIES:

1¾ CUPS (219 G) FLOUR

⅔ CUP (79 G) COCOA POWDER

2 TEASPOONS BAKING POWDER

1 TABLESPOON (8 G) CORNSTARCH

½ TEASPOON SALT

¼ TEASPOON CINNAMON

⅔ CUP (117 G) VEGAN CHOCOLATE CHIPS

1½ CUPS (300 G) SUGAR

½ CUP (120 ML) CANOLA OIL

1 TEASPOON VANILLA EXTRACT

⅔ CUP (160 ML) NONDAIRY MILK

FOR THE TOPPING:

1 BATCH CHOCOLATE MOUSSE (PAGE 166), MADE WITH COFFEE, WATER, OR NON-DAIRY MILK

⅓ CUP (16 G) VEGAN MARSHMALLOWS, CHOPPED

To make the brownies: Preheat oven to 350°F (180°C, or gas mark 4). Prepare an 8-inch (20.5 cm) square pan by greasing it or lining with parchment paper.

In a medium bowl, sift together the flour, cocoa powder, baking powder, cornstarch, salt, and cinnamon. Set aside.

Melt the chocolate chips in a glass bowl in the microwave, or on the stovetop using a double boiler over medium heat. In a large bowl, stir together the sugar, canola oil, melted chocolate, and vanilla. Pour in the milk and stir together until just combined.

Gradually add the dry ingredient mixture, stirring after each addition. Stir until almost completely smooth. It will be somewhat thin.

Pour into the prepared pan and bake for 25 to 30 minutes. Let cool in the pan.

To make the topping: Dollop or pipe on some Chocolate Mousse, then garnish with marshmallow pieces.

Root Beer Float Ice Cream Sandwiches

Graham crackers take root beer desserts to a new level when filled with sweet vanilla ice cream for an inspired ice cream sandwich.

YIELD: 10 ICE CREAM SANDWICHES

¾ CUP (94 G) ALL-PURPOSE FLOUR

1 CUP (125 G) WHOLE WHEAT PASTRY OR WHITE WHOLE WHEAT FLOUR

½ CUP (64 G) RYE FLOUR

½ CUP (100 G) SUGAR

1 TEASPOON BAKING POWDER

½ TEASPOON BAKING SODA

¼ TEASPOON CINNAMON

⅛ TEASPOON SALT

¼ CUP (56 G) VEGAN MARGARINE

3 TABLESPOONS (45 ML) AGAVE NECTAR OR MAPLE SYRUP

1 TABLESPOON (15 ML) DARK MOLASSES

1 TEASPOON CONCENTRATED ROOT BEER EXTRACT

3 TABLESPOONS (45 ML) NONDAIRY MILK PLUS 1 TABLESPOON (15 ML) RESERVED

1 TEASPOON VANILLA EXTRACT

1 QUART (570 G) NONDAIRY VANILLA ICE CREAM

In a large food processor, combine the flours, sugar, baking powder, baking soda, cinnamon, and salt. No need to sift.

Pulse until well blended. Add margarine, 1 tablespoon (14 g) at a time, and continue to process until the mix looks like small pebbles are scattered throughout.

Add agave nectar or maple syrup, molasses, root beer extract, 3 tablespoons (45 ml) milk, and vanilla extract. Process on medium until the dough collects into a ball, adding the remaining tablespoon of milk if the dough is too dry, plus more, if necessary.

Wrap the dough in plastic wrap and chill in the freezer for 25 minutes or in the fridge for a couple hours.

Preheat oven to 350°F (180°C, or gas mark 4).

Using a floured rolling pin, roll out the dough about ¼ inch (0.5 cm) thick on a floured surface, half at a time, if necessary.

Using a knife, cut dough into 2 x 4-inch (5 x 10 cm) rectangles or use cookie cutters for shapes. Place on a cookie sheet lined with parchment paper. With the knife, lightly score the grahams down the middle, widthwise. Poke them on both sides with a fork for the classic graham cracker appearance.

Bake for 15 to 18 minutes, until the edges are hard but not burned. The grahams won't be crunchy directly out of the oven, but will firm up when cool. Let cool completely.

Break the graham crackers in half so you have 2 halves. Scoop ¼ cup (36 g) ice cream onto one half, top with another half, then press together. Repeat for all the ice cream sandwiches. Store in the freezer.

Strawberry Milkshake Whoopie Pies

My favorite milkshake flavor is now in dessert form!

YIELD: 9 TO 10 WHOOPIE PIES

FOR THE PIES:
1 TEASPOON VINEGAR
½ CUP (120 ML) NONDAIRY MILK
¼ CUP (50 G) VEGAN SHORTENING
¼ CUP (56 G) VEGAN MARGARINE
1 CUP (200 G) SUGAR
¼ CUP (30 G) POWDERED SUGAR
⅓ CUP (82 G) APPLESAUCE
2 TEASPOONS STRAWBERRY EXTRACT
1 TEASPOON VANILLA EXTRACT
PINK FOOD COLORING (OPTIONAL)
2¼ CUPS (281 G) FLOUR
2½ TEASPOONS BAKING POWDER
¼ TEASPOON BAKING SODA
¼ TEASPOON SALT

FOR THE FILLING:
½ CUP (85 G) CHOPPED STRAWBERRIES
BASIC BUTTERCREAM (PAGE 168) OR
   1½ CUPS (353 ML) PREPARED VEGAN
   WHIPPED CREAM

To make the pies: Preheat oven to 375°F (190°C, or gas mark 5).

Add the vinegar to the milk and let sit for a few minutes, until curdled.

Cream together shortening and margarine. Add the sugar and continue mixing until thoroughly combined and fluffy.

Stir in powdered sugar and applesauce and continue beating.

Add the milk-vinegar mixture, strawberry and vanilla extracts, and food coloring (if using) and mix until completely incorporated.

Sift in the flour, baking powder, baking soda, and salt. Beat until all the flour is thoroughly mixed into the wet ingredients. The dough should be thick, lightweight, and fluffy. Refrigerate the dough for 15 to 20 minutes.

Using an ice cream scoop or a large spoon, drop about 3 table-spoons (45 g) of dough per whoopie pie half onto a cookie sheet lined with parchment paper. Repeat for 20 whoopie pie halves. Do not flatten. Bake for 12 to 14 minutes or until the tops are firm and the edges start to turn golden. Let cool.

To make the filling: Stir strawberries into the prepared butter-cream or whipped cream.

Spread a thick layer of buttercream or whipped cream on one half of a whoopie pie, and sandwich it together with another half. Repeat for all the whoopie pies.

Store in an airtight container in the fridge, separated. Like cup-cakes, these whoopie pies have a tendency to stick together and rip apart if stored on top of each other.

Root Beer Float Whoopie Pies

Soft, cakelike root beer–flavored cookie halves encase a sweet vanilla ice cream filling in these whoopie pies.

YIELD: 8 OR 9 WHOOPIE PIES
---

1 CUP (235 ML) NONDAIRY MILK

1 TEASPOON VINEGAR

⅓ CUP (80 ML) CANOLA OIL

½ CUP (100 G) SUGAR

½ CUP (115 G) BROWN SUGAR

1 TABLESPOON (8 G) CORNSTARCH

½ TEASPOON VANILLA EXTRACT

1½ TEASPOONS CONCENTRATED ROOT BEER EXTRACT

2¼ CUPS (281 G) FLOUR

1½ TEASPOONS COCOA POWDER

1 TEASPOON BAKING SODA

½ TEASPOON SALT

1 QUART (570 G) NONDAIRY VANILLA ICE CREAM

Preheat oven to 350°F (180°C, or gas mark 4).

Pour the milk and vinegar into a medium bowl and let sit to curdle for about 5 minutes. Add the canola oil, sugars, cornstarch, and extracts and mix completely.

Sift in the flour, cocoa powder, baking soda, and salt and mix until the dry ingredients are completely incorporated. The dough should be somewhat thick and very tacky.

Line a cookie sheet with parchment paper, then using a cookie or ice cream scoop, drop about 2 tablespoons (32 g) of dough per pie half onto the cookie sheet, leaving about 3 inches in between pies and the edges of the pan.

Bake for 10 to 12 minutes or until the tops are firm. Transfer to a wire rack to cool.

Stick the tray of pies in the freezer for 5 to 10 minutes and take out the ice cream to soften.

Take the pies out of the freezer and scoop about ⅓ cup (48 g) ice cream onto one half, then top with another half. Repeat for all the pies. Do this quickly if you're working in warm weather. Return the finished pies to the freezer so the ice cream can firm up more, then serve! Store in the freezer.

RECIPE NOTES
- If you can find cream soda extract, replace the root beer extract for cream soda float pies!
- If you want a little more root beer flavor, blend ½ teaspoon (2.5 ml) root beer extract into the ice cream in a stand mixer or with a spoon. Stick the bowl of ice cream back in the freezer if it begins to melt.

Fried Coca-Cola

Originating at the State Fair of Texas, fried Coke is deep-fried Coca-Cola batter topped with Coca-Cola syrup, whipped cream, cinnamon sugar, and a cherry.

YIELD: 4 TO 6 SERVINGS

FOR THE SYRUP:

¾ CUP (150 G) SUGAR

2 TEASPOONS COCOA POWDER

3 OUNCES (90 ML) COCA-COLA

¼ CUP (56 G) VEGAN MARGARINE

1 TABLESPOON (15 ML) LIGHT CORN SYRUP

½ TEASPOON VANILLA EXTRACT

⅛ TEASPOON COLA EXTRACT

FOR THE BATTER:

1 TABLESPOON (8 G) CORNSTARCH

½ CUP (120 ML) NONDAIRY MILK

2 CUPS (250 G) FLOUR

1 TEASPOON BAKING POWDER

¼ TEASPOON SALT

3 TABLESPOONS (39 G) SUGAR

2 TEASPOONS LIGHT CORN SYRUP

2 TABLESPOONS (25 G) VEGAN SHORTENING, MELTED

1¼ CUPS (295 ML) COCA-COLA

½ TEASPOON VANILLA EXTRACT

FOR THE TOPPINGS:

PREPARED VEGAN WHIPPED CREAM OR COCONUT WHIPPED CREAM (PAGE 167)

CINNAMON

POWDERED SUGAR

MARASCHINO CHERRIES

To make the syrup: Mix sugar, cocoa, 2¼ ounces (67 ml) of the cola, margarine, and corn syrup in a saucepan. Bring to boil over medium heat. Stir constantly until thickened, 7 to 9 minutes. Add rest of the cola after 4 minutes.

Remove from heat and stir in extracts. Set aside. If syrup becomes too thick as it cools, stir in additional Coca-Cola until it reaches syrup consistency.

To make the batter: Dissolve cornstarch in the milk. Heat mixture in a saucepan over medium heat until it thickens. Set aside to cool.

Combine flour, baking powder, and salt in a mixing bowl. Make a well in the center and add remaining ingredients and cornstarch mixture. Whisk until smooth. It should be thin, like pancake batter, but not watery. Chill for 15 minutes.

Fill a large pot halfway with oil and heat to 350°F (180°C). Once a bit of batter dropped into the oil rises and bubbles, it's ready. Place a cooling rack over a cookie sheet lined with paper towels to catch drips.

Use a large spoon to drizzle ⅓ cup (80 ml) batter at a time into the hot oil in a circular motion. Fry for 1 to 2 minutes, flip with metal tongs, then fry for another minute. Place on cooling rack. The first couple times may be practice until you get the hang of it.

To assemble: Fill bowls with fried Coca-Cola, drizzle syrup on top, then top with whipped cream, cinnamon, powdered sugar, and a cherry. Grab a fork and dig in!

RECIPE NOTES
- Cola extract can be found in cake decorating stores, craft stores, and online.
- For a Fried Root Beer Float, replace Coca-Cola and cola extract with root beer and root beer extract. Top with ice cream instead of whipped cream.

Chocolate Malt Shakes

Superrich coconut cream is the base of this shake, making it as thick and creamy as possible. If you're not a fan of coconut, the chocolate and malt syrup completely mask the coconut flavor.

YIELD: 1 OR 2 SERVINGS

FOR 1 SHAKE:

1 CAN (15 OUNCES OR 440 ML) FULL-FAT
COCONUT MILK

⅓ CUP (40 G) POWDERED SUGAR

½ TEASPOON VANILLA EXTRACT

2½ TABLESPOONS (37.5 ML) BARLEY
MALT SYRUP

¼ CUP (30 G) COCOA POWDER

1 CUP (235 ML) ALMOND MILK, TO START

FOR 2 SHAKES:

2 CANS (15 OUNCES OR 440 ML EACH)
FULL-FAT COCONUT MILK

⅔ CUP (80 G) POWDERED SUGAR

1 TEASPOON VANILLA EXTRACT

5 TABLESPOONS (75 ML) BARLEY MALT
SYRUP

½ CUP (59 G) COCOA POWDER

2 CUPS (470 ML) ALMOND MILK, TO
START

Let the can of coconut milk sit undisturbed for a few days, then transfer to the refrigerator. Let chill overnight.

Open the can and scoop out the cream that has risen to the top. Combine the cream, powdered sugar, and vanilla extract in a mixing bowl and whip. If you'd like to top your shake with whipped coconut cream, set aside a tablespoon or two of this whipped cream.

Stir in the barley malt syrup and cocoa powder. Transfer this mixture to a smaller container and place in the freezer until it thickens up, but do not let it freeze completely. Even better, put it in an ice cream maker if you have one.

After 2 hours, remove the container from the freezer and stir it up until it takes on the consistency of soft-serve ice cream.

Transfer this mixture to a blender. Add the almond milk and blend. Taste, then add more barley malt if you want a more prominent flavor. Continue adding almond milk until the shake reaches desired consistency.

Drizzle malt syrup around the inside of a glass, then pour in the milkshake and top with whipped cream and a cherry!

RECIPE NOTE
If you'd prefer to just eat chocolate malt ice cream, stop after the freezing step and serve.

Malted Milk Chocolate Cake

The complex flavor of malted milk lends a rich flavor to fluffy chocolate cake.

YIELD: 8 TO 12 SERVINGS

FOR THE CAKE:

⅔ CUP (160 ML) CANOLA OIL

½ CUP (120 ML) BARLEY MALT SYRUP

1 CUP (200 G) SUGAR

1¾ CUPS (411 ML) ALMOND MILK

1 TEASPOON VANILLA EXTRACT

2 TEASPOONS APPLE CIDER VINEGAR

2½ CUPS (312 G) FLOUR

¾ CUP (89 G) COCOA POWDER

2 TEASPOONS BAKING SODA

½ TEASPOON SALT

FOR THE FROSTING:

½ CUP (112 G) VEGAN MARGARINE

½ CUP (100 G) VEGAN SHORTENING

3 TO 4 TABLESPOONS (45 TO 60 ML)
   BARLEY MALT SYRUP

3 CUPS (360 G) POWDERED SUGAR

¼ CUP (30 G) COCOA POWDER

1 TO 2 TABLESPOONS (15 TO 30 ML)
   ALMOND MILK

To make the cake: Preheat oven to 325°F (170°C, or gas mark 3).

Line two 8-inch (20.5 cm) round cake pans with parchment and grease the sides with vegan margarine or cooking spray. Set aside.

Put the canola oil, barley malt syrup, sugar, almond milk, vanilla extract, and apple cider vinegar in a stand mixer or large mixing bowl. Stir until just combined. Make sure the barley malt syrup is incorporated into the mixture.

Combine the flour, cocoa powder, baking soda, and salt in a separate bowl. Gradually sift into the wet ingredients, stirring after each addition. The batter should be thick and pourable.

Divide the batter evenly between the cake pans. Bake for 34 to 36 minutes, until the tops of the cakes are firm and a toothpick inserted in the center comes out clean. Transfer the pans to a wire rack to cool before attempting to remove the cakes from their pans.

To make the frosting: Cream together the margarine, shortening, and barley malt syrup in a stand mixer or with hand beaters.

Gradually add the powdered sugar and cocoa, stirring as you go. Mix until completely incorporated, then add the almond milk. If the frosting is too soft or liquid, add more powdered sugar. Beat the frosting for 6 to 8 minutes. Add more powdered sugar, barley malt, or almond milk to adjust the flavor and consistency of the frosting, if necessary.

Remove the cakes from the pans. Spread frosting atop one cake and place the second cake on top. Frost the sides and top of the double-layer cake, piping on a border or adding chocolate and candy for decoration if desired.

CHAPTER 6

the holiday table

These recipes grasp inspiration from holidays throughout the year and traditional drinks from around the world.

Mojito Wedding Cookies

Traditional Mexican wedding cookies dressed up with lime, mint, and a touch of rum for a mojito in a cookie.

YIELD: 20 TO 22 COOKIES

1½ CUPS (180 G) POWDERED SUGAR
⅔ CUP (150 G) VEGAN MARGARINE
½ TEASPOON RUM EXTRACT
2 TEASPOONS RUM
2 TEASPOONS LIME JUICE
1 TEASPOON LIME ZEST
1 TABLESPOON (6 G) CHOPPED FRESH
   MINT
¼ TEASPOON SALT
2 CUPS (250 G) FLOUR

Preheat oven to 350°F (180°C, or gas mark 4).

Cream together the powdered sugar and margarine in a bowl or stand mixer. Add in the rum extract, rum, lime juice, lime zest, mint, and salt, and stir until smooth.

Sift in the flour and mix the dough until combined.

Roll into 1-inch (2.5 cm) balls and place on a cookie sheet lined with parchment paper. Bake for 15 minutes or until the bottoms start turning golden and the tops of the cookies are firming up. Transfer to a wire rack to cool.

REPLACING THE ALCOHOL
Replace the rum with an additional ¼ teaspoon rum extract.

Chocolate Nog Cupcakes

Vegan eggnog can be found in traditional and specialty grocery stores during the holiday season. Eggnog cupcakes deserve a place alongside the peppermint, anise, and spicy flavors of the holiday dessert table.

YIELD: 12 CUPCAKES

FOR THE CUPCAKES:

1 CUP (235 ML) VEGAN EGGNOG

1 TEASPOON APPLE CIDER VINEGAR

¾ CUP (150 G) SUGAR

⅓ CUP (80 ML) CANOLA OIL

¼ TEASPOON VANILLA EXTRACT

½ TEASPOON RUM EXTRACT

2 TABLESPOONS (30 ML) RUM

1¼ CUPS (156 G) FLOUR

⅓ CUP (40 ML) COCOA POWDER

¾ TEASPOON BAKING SODA

½ TEASPOON BAKING POWDER

¼ TEASPOON SALT

¾ TEASPOON FRESHLY GRATED NUTMEG

FOR THE FROSTING:

⅓ CUP (67 G) VEGAN SHORTENING

⅓ CUP (75 G) VEGAN MARGARINE

2½ CUPS (300 G) POWDERED SUGAR

3 TABLESPOONS (45 ML) VEGAN EGGNOG

¼ TEASPOON RUM EXTRACT

¼ TEASPOON FRESHLY GRATED NUTMEG

To make cupcakes: Preheat oven to 350°F (180°C, or gas mark 4). Line a cupcake pan with 12 liners.

Combine vegan eggnog and vinegar and set aside for 3 minutes to curdle.

Stir together eggnog-vinegar mixture, sugar, oil, extracts, and rum in a large mixing bowl.

Sift in flour, cocoa powder, baking soda, baking powder, salt, and nutmeg. Whisk together until just combined.

Fill cupcake liners halfway with batter. Bake for 18 minutes, or until the tops are firm. Transfer to a wire rack to cool.

To make frosting: Cream together shortening and margarine Gradually sift in powdered sugar, mixing as you go. Add in eggnog, rum extract, and nutmeg.

Whip frosting with a hand or stand mixer for 6 to 8 minutes, until fluffy.

Pipe or spread frosting on cooled cupcakes. Garnish with sprinkles or candy canes.

REPLACING THE ALCOHOL
Replace the rum with an additional ¼ teaspoon rum extract.

Strawberry Champagne Truffles

Ring in the New Year with rich chocolate truffles with a burst of strawberry and Champagne flavor.

YIELD: 15 TO 20 TRUFFLES

2 CUPS (350 G) VEGAN CHOCOLATE CHIPS
½ CUP (120 ML) CHAMPAGNE
1 TABLESPOON (15 ML) ALMOND MILK
2 TABLESPOONS (40 G) STRAWBERRY JAM
1 TEASPOON COCOA POWDER
¼ CUP (56 G) VEGAN MARGARINE
COCOA POWDER, FOR ROLLING

Melt chocolate, Champagne, and almond milk together in a double boiler over medium heat or in a glass bowl in the microwave. Pour mixture into a bowl if necessary. Mix until completely smooth and set aside to cool.

Fill another bowl with 7 or 8 cubes of ice and 1 cup (235 ml) water.

Place the bowl filled with the melted chocolate into the ice bath. Using electric beaters on high speed, start whipping up the chocolate evenly around the bowl. Add the strawberry jam, cocoa powder, and margarine, and continue whipping.

You will see bubbles forming everywhere, and the chocolate mixture will start to thicken up to the consistency of heavy cream after a few minutes. Continue whipping for another 2 minutes, until the consistency becomes very thick. Avoid over-whipping, which could cause the filling to become soft and collapse or become grainy.

Remove the first bowl from the ice bath. Cover the bowl with plastic wrap and place in the refrigerator to let the chocolate chill and thicken. Prepare a baking sheet with parchment paper or a silicone mat, and pour about ¼ cup (30 g) cocoa powder into a shallow bowl.

Remove the mixture from the refrigerator. Using a small cookie scoop, make balls that are about 1 inch (2.5 cm) in diameter, then roll in the cocoa powder and place on the baking sheet.

Place the tray of rolled truffles in the refrigerator for at least 1 hour, then eat! Keep stored in refrigerator in an airtight container for up to 2 weeks.

Mini Pumpkin Apple Rum Pies

These mini pumpkin apple pies combine the best parts of each pie: pumpkin filling, apple filling on top, and minimal crust. The pumpkin filling is adapted from the notoriously perfect pumpkin pecan pie recipe from Myra Kornfield's *Voluptuous Vegan*.

YIELD: 12 MINI PIES

FOR THE CRUST:

2 CUPS (250 G) FLOUR

¾ TEASPOON BAKING POWDER

¼ TEASPOON SALT

2 TABLESPOONS (26 G) SUGAR

⅓ CUP (75 G) COCONUT OIL

⅓ CUP (80 ML) COLD WATER

1 TEASPOON APPLE CIDER VINEGAR

2 TABLESPOONS (30 ML) VODKA

FOR THE FILLING:

1 CAN (15 OUNCES OR 490 G) PUMPKIN PURÉE

⅓ CUP (80 ML) MAPLE SYRUP

⅓ CUP (80 ML) CANNED COCONUT MILK

1 TABLESPOON (14 G) COCONUT OIL

¾ TEASPOON CINNAMON

½ TEASPOON GROUND GINGER

⅛ TEASPOON FRESHLY GRATED NUTMEG

¼ TEASPOON SALT

4 TEASPOONS CORNSTARCH

¾ TEASPOON AGAR POWDER

FOR THE TOPPING:

1 TEASPOON VEGAN MARGARINE

2 TEASPOONS COCONUT OIL

2 APPLES, PEELED AND CHOPPED INTO
   ½-INCH (1.5 CM) PIECES

¼ CUP (60 G) BROWN SUGAR

¼ TEASPOON CINNAMON

2 TABLESPOONS (30 ML) RUM

½ TEASPOON VANILLA EXTRACT

½ CUP (32 G) RAW PUMPKIN SEEDS

1 TABLESPOON (15 ML) VEGETABLE OIL

1 TEASPOON SALT

¼ TEASPOON CINNAMON

FRESHLY GROUND BLACK PEPPER, TO TASTE

1 BATCH COCONUT WHIPPED CREAM
   (PAGE 167)

Preheat oven to 350°F (180°C, or gas mark 4).

To make the crust: Place flour, baking powder, salt, and sugar into a large bowl and cut in coconut oil (a solid at room temperature) until dough resembles pebbles.

Add water, vinegar, and vodka and mix until completely incorporated. Roll golf ball–sized pieces of dough into 3-inch (7.5 cm) circles. Press into cupcake pan cups.

To make the filling: Combine all ingredients in a food processor and blend until smooth.

Fill each crust with filling. Cover pan with foil and bake for 40 to 45 minutes.

Let the pies sit in the pan for 15 to 20 minutes. Loosen edges, then remove from the pan and transfer to cooling rack.

To make the topping: Melt margarine and oil in a pan over medium heat and toss in apples, stirring to coat. Add brown sugar, cinnamon, and 1 tablespoon (15 ml) of the rum. Lower heat and continue to cook, stirring frequently, for 5 to 6 minutes, until the mixture is syrupy.

Add remaining rum while apples are cooking. Remove from heat and stir in vanilla.

Coat pumpkin seeds in the vegetable oil and toss with the salt, cinnamon, and pepper. Scatter onto a baking sheet and toast in the oven for 10 minutes, or until fragrant, stirring halfway through.

Top pies with a spoonful of apples, a dollop of coconut whipped cream, and a sprinkle of pumpkin seeds.

Mexican Hot Chocolate Gelato with Cinnamon Sugar Tortilla Strips

Mexican hot chocolate—spicy, rich, and chocolaty. Ice cream is the perfect vehicle for these flavors and sensations. Like sweet and salty or spicy and sweet, the heat of the chile powder is quite a treat in a frozen dessert that's topped with a churro-like garnish.

YIELD: 1 PINT (285 G)

FOR THE GELATO:

1 CAN (15 OUNCES OR 440 ML) COCONUT MILK

1 CINNAMON STICK

¼ CUP (30 G) COCOA POWDER

½ CUP (100 G) SUGAR

2 WEDGES (22.5 G) MEXICAN DRINKING CHOCOLATE

⅛ TEASPOON CINNAMON

¾ TO 1 TEASPOON GROUND CHILE POWDER

⅛ TO ¼ TEASPOON CAYENNE PEPPER

PINCH OF SALT

½ TEASPOON VANILLA EXTRACT

FOR THE STRIPS:

5 FLOUR TORTILLAS (6 INCHES OR 15 CM IN DIAMETER)

2 TABLESPOONS (28 G) MELTED MARGA-RINE OR VEGETABLE OIL

1 TEASPOON CINNAMON

¼ CUP (50 G) SUGAR

To make the gelato: Combine all ingredients except for the vanilla in a saucepan over medium heat and whisk until the cocoa, sugar, and drinking chocolate dissolve, about 5 minutes.

Start out with the smaller amount of chile powder and cayenne, then taste and adjust the spices and heat level if necessary. Remove from heat and stir in the vanilla extract.

Let cool completely, remove the cinnamon stick, then freeze in an ice cream maker according to the manufacturer's instructions.

To make the strips: Preheat oven to 350°F (180°C, or gas mark 4).

Brush both sides of each tortilla with the melted margarine. Stack on a cutting board and cut into ½-inch (1 cm) strips lengthwise, then cut the longer pieces in half widthwise.

Combine the cinnamon and sugar in a gallon-sized zip-top bag. Place the tortilla strips in the bag, seal the top, and shake until the strips are coated in cinnamon sugar. The shaking will separate all the pieces that are stuck together.

Scatter all the strips out on a parchment-lined baking sheet and bake until golden, crispy, bubbly, and wavy, 12 to 14 minutes, stirring them at the 10-minute mark.

Serve gelato garnished with cinnamon sugar tortilla strips and perhaps a dollop of dairy-free whipped cream. Leftover cinnamon strips are great for snacking!

Margarita Ice Cream

Serve in salt-rimmed glasses garnished with a slice of lime! Alcohol and salt are two of the main ingredients in a margarita, but they will melt ice cream, so don't be tempted to add extra of either.

YIELD: 1 PINT (285 G)

1 CAN (15 OUNCES OR 440 ML)
   COCONUT MILK
⅓ CUP (80 ML) AGAVE NECTAR
⅓ CUP (80 ML) LIME JUICE
1 TEASPOON LIME ZEST
¼ CUP (60 ML) TEQUILA
¼ TEASPOON ORANGE EXTRACT
¼ TEASPOON SALT

Stir all ingredients together in a bowl and freeze in an ice cream maker according to the manufacturer's instructions.

RECIPE NOTE
Prepare salt-rimmed glasses by rubbing a slice of lime around the outside edge of each glass, then roll the edge around in a plate of salt. Tap the glass to remove excess salt. Avoid getting salt on the inside of glass as it will drip into the ice cream.

White Chocolate Nog Truffles

Looking for something to do with the last bit of vegan eggnog in a carton? Whip up these white chocolate truffles that showcase the flavors and richness of the drink.

YIELD: 24 TRUFFLES

1½ CUPS (263 G) VEGAN WHITE
   CHOCOLATE CHIPS

¼ CUP (56 G) VEGAN MARGARINE

½ TEASPOON RUM EXTRACT

3 TABLESPOONS (45 ML) VEGAN EGGNOG

½ CUP (60 G) POWDERED SUGAR

HEAPING ¼ TEASPOON FRESHLY GRATED
   NUTMEG

2 CUPS (350 G) VEGAN CHOCOLATE CHIPS

1 TABLESPOON (12.5 G) VEGAN SHORTENING

Melt the white chocolate chips in a double boiler over medium heat or in a glass bowl in the microwave, then transfer to a medium bowl.

Stir in the margarine, rum extract, and vegan eggnog. Let cool, popping the mixture in the freezer if necessary to prevent the powdered sugar from melting. Stir in the powdered sugar and nutmeg.

The mixture should be thick and not too sticky. Powder your hands with extra powdered sugar and roll into ¾-inch (2 cm) balls. If the mixture isn't holding together, add a few more tablespoons of powdered sugar to the mixture. Place balls on a silicone mat or parchment-lined baking sheet and freeze until firm.

Melt the chocolate chips and shortening together in a double boiler over medium heat or in a glass bowl in the microwave. Dip the truffles into the chocolate-shortening mixture, then remove with a fork and place them back onto the baking sheet. Repeat with each truffle and return to the freezer so they can firm up. If the white chocolate starts to melt while you are dipping the truffles, dust with powdered sugar and re-roll the balls, then freeze again before continuing to dip them.

When you remove the truffles from the freezer, patch up any spots that didn't get covered with the leftover chocolate.

RECIPE NOTE
Vegan eggnog out of season? Most of the eggnog flavor in this recipe comes from the nutmeg and rum extract, so you can replace the vegan eggnog with any nondairy milk, even in July.

Buttered Rum Cashew Brittle

The rich flavors of butter and rum become an addictive, crunchy treat!

YIELD: 18 PIECES
---

1 CUP (200 G) SUGAR
½ CUP (115 G) BROWN SUGAR
⅓ CUP LIGHT CORN SYRUP OR BROWN
   RICE SYRUP
½ CUP (112 G) VEGAN MARGARINE
½ TEASPOON CINNAMON
⅛ TEASPOON FRESHLY GRATED NUTMEG
PINCH OF GROUND CLOVES
¼ TEASPOON SALT
3 TABLESPOONS (45 ML) WATER
½ TEASPOON BAKING SODA
2 TEASPOONS RUM EXTRACT
1⅓ CUPS (195 G) ROASTED SALTED
   CASHEWS

Line a cookie sheet with parchment paper. Set aside.

Prepare a cup of cold water to test your brittle if you're not using a candy thermometer.

Combine the sugar, brown sugar, corn syrup, margarine, spices, salt, and water in medium saucepan.

Turn heat to medium and cook, stirring frequently, until the mixture reaches 300°F (150°C, or gas mark 2), 11 to 12 minutes. If you don't have a candy thermometer, drop a spoonful of the mixture into a cup of cold water. If the mixture turns into crunchy threads, you're at the correct temperature.

Remove from heat, then stir in the baking soda, rum extract, and cashews. Immediately pour onto the cookie sheet and let cool. When the brittle hardens, break into pieces. Store in an airtight container for up to 1 month.

Orange Liqueur Chocolate Truffles ▶

A cross between a rum ball and a truffle, these dreamy chocolates with a hint of orange are perfect for the winter months.

YIELD: 20 TO 24 TRUFFLES

⅓ CUP (80 ML) FULL-FAT COCONUT MILK
1 PACKAGE (12 OUNCES OR 340 G) VEGAN
   SEMISWEET CHOCOLATE CHIPS
¼ CUP (30 G) COCOA POWDER
¼ CUP (28 G) CHOCOLATE COOKIE
   CRUMBS
¼ CUP (60 ML) GRAND MARNIER
1 TEASPOON ORANGE ZEST
POWDERED SUGAR OR COCOA, FOR ROLLING

Melt the coconut milk and chocolate together in a double boiler over medium heat, or in a glass bowl in the microwave. Stir until smooth.

Add the cocoa, cookie crumbs, Grand Marnier, and orange zest. Cover and chill in the refrigerator for 5 to 6 hours, or overnight.

Sprinkle a large plate with a layer of powdered sugar or cocoa for rolling.

Scoop out chocolate with a tablespoon, roll into balls, and roll around in the powdered sugar to coat. Don't worry if the chocolate is very thick or difficult to scoop. This prevents it from melting into a chocolaty mess while rolling between your palms.

Place truffles in mini cupcake liners. Store in the refrigerator before serving.

CHAPTER 7

the bar

Dark, relaxing, no-frills drinks gradually melt into lush pastries. Try malted beer brownies or autumnal pumpkin beer bread, then get your vino on with Chardonnay or Cabernet. You'll be toasting with (or perhaps to) these sweet treats in no time!

Malted Beer Brownies

Two kinds of malt in are one simple, hardy brownie.

YIELD: 9 TO 12 BROWNIES

1¾ CUPS (219 G) FLOUR
⅔ CUP (79 G) COCOA POWDER
2 TEASPOONS BAKING POWDER
1 TABLESPOON (8 G) CORNSTARCH
½ TEASPOON SALT
½ CUP (88 G) VEGAN CHOCOLATE CHIPS
1¼ CUPS (250 G) SUGAR
½ CUP (120 ML) CANOLA OIL
1 TEASPOON VANILLA EXTRACT
⅔ CUP (160 ML) BEER
⅓ CUP (80 ML) BARLEY MALT SYRUP

Preheat oven to 350°F (180°C, or gas mark 4). Prepare an 8-inch (20.5 cm) square pan by greasing it or lining with parchment paper.

In a medium bowl, sift together flour, cocoa powder, baking powder, cornstarch, and salt. Set aside.

Melt the chocolate in a double boiler over medium heat or in a glass bowl in the microwave. In a large bowl, stir together the sugar, canola oil, melted chocolate, and vanilla.

Pour in the beer and stir until just combined. You'll need to work quickly after adding the beer so it doesn't lose too much carbonation before baking.

Drizzle in the barley malt syrup and stir until incorporated. This mixture will be very thick and sticky after adding the syrup.

Gradually add the dry ingredient mixture, stirring after each addition until almost completely smooth. It will be somewhat thin.

Pour into the prepared pan and bake for 25 to 30 minutes. Let cool in the pan, then cut and serve!

Coffee Stout Salted Caramels

Beer and coffee add another dimension to chewy salted caramels. I like using coffee extract because it adds a pleasant coffee flavor without changing the texture or adding excessive moisture.

⅓ CUP (75 G) VEGAN MARGARINE
¾ CUP (170 G) BROWN SUGAR
⅓ CUP (80 ML) DARK BEER OR STOUT
¼ CUP (60 ML) LIGHT CORN SYRUP OR
   BROWN RICE SYRUP
1 TEASPOON SALT
¾ TEASPOON VANILLA EXTRACT
½ TEASPOON COFFEE EXTRACT

Line an 8 x 4-inch (20 x 10 cm) loaf pan with parchment paper. Set aside.

Combine all ingredients in a medium saucepan and bring to a simmer over medium heat.

Stirring frequently, cook the mixture to soft ball stage, which is 238°F (114°C), or when a spoonful dropped into a bowl of cold water holds it shape and feels like a squishy, pliable ball, 10 to 12 minutes.

Cook for an additional 30 seconds at soft ball stage, then immediately remove from heat.

Pour mixture into prepared pan and let cool. Slice into 1½ x ½-inch (4 x 1.5 cm) rectangles (or any size you want). Wrap in foil squares, or eat directly out of the pan.

RECIPE NOTE
If you like your salted caramels saltier, feel free to add up to ½ teaspoon more salt.

Coconut Stout S'mores Cupcakes

Traditional s'mores grow up with coconut and stout, all wrapped up in a cupcake.

FOR THE CUPCAKES:

1 CUP (235 ML) CHOCOLATE STOUT

1 TABLESPOON (15 ML) COCONUT
   VINEGAR OR APPLE CIDER VINEGAR

1 CUP (200 G) SUGAR

¼ CUP (60 ML) CANOLA OIL

2 TABLESPOONS (28 G) COCONUT OIL

¾ TEASPOON VANILLA EXTRACT

1¼ CUPS (156 G) FLOUR

½ CUP (59 G) COCOA POWDER

2 TEASPOONS BAKING SODA

¼ TEASPOON SALT

½ CUP (43 G) FLAKED COCONUT

FOR GARNISH:

BASIC BUTTERCREAM (PAGE 168)

GRAHAM CRACKERS

MARSHMALLOWS

VEGAN CHOCOLATE CHIPS

FLAKED COCONUT

To make the cupcakes: Preheat oven to 350°F (180°C, or gas mark 4). Prepare a cupcake pan with 12 liners.

Pour the stout and vinegar into a stand mixer or regular mixing bowl. Stir in the sugar, oils, and vanilla extract.

Sift in the flour, cocoa powder, baking soda, and salt, and mix until almost combined. Stir in the coconut. The batter should be thick but pourable.

Using an ice cream scoop or large spoon, fill each liner two-thirds full. Bake for 18 minutes, or until the tops are firm and a tooth-pick inserted in the center comes out clean.

Let sit in the pan on the stove for 3 to 4 minutes, then move to a cooling rack to cool completely.

To garnish: Pipe or spread the Basic Buttercream frosting on the cupcakes, then garnish with graham crackers, marshmallows, chocolate, and flaked coconut as desired.

Coconut Rum-and-Coke Cupcakes

These cupcakes are great for lounging whilst welcoming the summer months. Coconut cream and milk are utilized in this recipe, adding a tropical spin on rum and coke. To further the tropical theme, rum-caramelized bananas are added as a variation!

YIELD: 12 CUPCAKES

FOR THE CUPCAKES:
⅓ CUP (75 G) VEGAN MARGARINE
⅓ CUP (80 ML) COCONUT CREAM (PAGE 168)
½ CUP (115 G) BROWN SUGAR
⅓ CUP (67 G) SUGAR
⅓ CUP (80 ML) COCONUT MILK (FROM A
   CARTON, NOT A CAN)
2 TEASPOONS VANILLA EXTRACT
2 TABLESPOONS (30 ML) DARK RUM
1½ CUPS (188 G) FLOUR
2 TEASPOONS BAKING POWDER
½ TEASPOON SALT

FOR THE FROSTING:
⅓ CUP (80 ML) COCONUT CREAM (PAGE 168)
⅓ CUP (67 G) VEGAN SHORTENING
¼ CUP (56 G) VEGAN MARGARINE
2 CUPS (240 G) POWDERED SUGAR
¾ TEASPOON LEMON ZEST
½ TO ¾ TEASPOON COLA EXTRACT
¼ TEASPOON RUM EXTRACT

To make the cupcakes: Preheat oven to 350°F (180°C, or gas mark 4) and line a cupcake pan with 12 liners.

Cream the margarine, coconut cream, brown sugar, and sugar together with a stand mixer or handheld beaters. Stir in milk, vanilla, and rum.

Sift in flour, baking powder, and salt and mix until just combined. The batter should be dark and somewhat thick.

Using an ice cream scoop or large spoon, fill each cupcake liner halfway. Bake for about 18 minutes, or until the tops are firm. Let cool in the tray for 5 to 10 minutes, then transfer to a wire rack to cool completely.

To make the frosting: Cream together the coconut cream, shortening, and margarine in a stand mixer or with electric beaters. Gradually add the powdered sugar until completely incorporated.

Add the lemon zest, cola extract, and rum extract and continue beating until extremely smooth and fluffy, 6 to 8 minutes. Adjust flavors to taste.

Fill pastry bag with the frosting and swirl atop the cupcakes. Store in the refrigerator and take out 15 minutes before serving.

RECIPE NOTE
These cupcakes are fabulous accompanied with Bananas Foster á la Mode (page 157). Eat alongside the cupcakes, or use as garnish.

REPLACING THE ALCOHOL
Use ¾ teaspoon rum extract instead of dark rum in the cupcakes.

Jack and Cake

Have your Jack and Coke in a cake! A touch of lemon brightens up this classic drink in chocolate cake form.

YIELD: 12 TO 16 SERVINGS

FOR THE CAKE:

2 ⅔ CUPS (333 G) FLOUR
⅔ CUP (79 G) COCOA POWDER
1½ CUPS (300 G) SUGAR
2 TEASPOONS BAKING SODA
½ TEASPOON SALT
⅔ CUP (160 ML) CANOLA OIL
1¾ CUPS (411 ML) COLA
⅓ CUP (80 ML) NONDAIRY MILK
3 TABLESPOONS (45 ML) WHISKEY
1 TEASPOON VANILLA EXTRACT
1 TEASPOON COLA EXTRACT
2 TEASPOONS APPLE CIDER VINEGAR

FOR THE FROSTING:

½ CUP (112 G) VEGAN MARGARINE
½ CUP (100 G) VEGAN SHORTENING
3 CUPS (360 ML) POWDERED SUGAR
½ CUP (59 G) COCOA POWDER
½ TEASPOON COLA EXTRACT
3 TABLESPOONS (45 ML) WHISKEY
1 TABLESPOON (15 ML) LEMON JUICE

To make the cake: Preheat oven to 350°F (180°C, or gas mark 4). Line with parchment paper or grease two 8-inch (20.5 cm) round cake pans.

Combine the flour, cocoa powder, sugar, baking soda, and salt in a stand mixer or mixing bowl. Stir until combined.

Create a well in the center of the dry ingredients and add the canola oil, cola, milk, whiskey, vanilla extract, cola extract, and apple cider vinegar. Mix until combined.

Fill each cake pan halfway full. Bake for 25 to 28 minutes, until the tops of the cakes are firm and a toothpick inserted in the center comes out clean. Transfer to a wire rack to cool.

To make the frosting: Cream together margarine and shortening in a stand mixer or with hand beaters.

Gradually add the powdered sugar and cocoa, sifting as you go. Halfway through, add the cola extract, whiskey, and lemon juice.

Mix until completely incorporated, and beat the frosting for 6 to 8 minutes. Add more powdered sugar or milk to adjust the consistency of the frosting if necessary.

Frost the top of one cake, place the second cake on top, then frost the entire layered cake. Pipe on a border with a pastry bag, if desired. Garnish with lemon slices and dark chocolate.

Gingerbread Stout Cake with Irish Buttercream

A classic gingerbread with the addition of beer elevates this dessert to star of the table with creamy Irish whiskey frosting.

To make the cake: Preheat oven to 350°F (180°C, or gas mark 4). Line a 9-inch (23 cm) square pan with parchment or grease with oil.

Combine the sugars, molasses, applesauce or yogurt, and oil in a bowl or stand mixer and stir to combine. Combine the milk and lemon juice and let sit for several minutes to curdle, then add to the mixture.

Sift in the flours, cocoa, baking soda, cinnamon, ginger, nutmeg, cloves, and salt and stir until partially combined. Gradually whisk in the beer, mixing until just combined, and all the lumps are mixed in.

Pour the batter into the pan and bake for 30 minutes. Transfer the pan to a cooling rack. After 10 to 15 minutes, loosen the edges with a knife, but don't remove from the pan, and let cool completely.

To make the frosting: Cream together the shortening and margarine in a stand mixer or using a hand mixer. Gradually add the powdered sugar while mixing.

Add the cocoa, whiskey, vanilla, coffee extract, and milk and whip until light and fluffy, 6 to 8 minutes. If it's too thick, add more milk, or add powdered sugar if it's too thin.

While the cake is still in the pan, spread the frosting on the cake in an even layer, then cut and serve.

YIELD: 9 TO 12 SERVINGS

FOR THE CAKE:

⅓ CUP (67 G) SUGAR

⅓ CUP (75 G) BROWN SUGAR

⅓ CUP (80 ML) DARK MOLASSES

½ CUP (125 G) APPLESAUCE OR NONDAIRY YOGURT

½ CUP (120 ML) CANOLA OIL

½ CUP (120 ML) NONDAIRY MILK

1 TABLESPOON (15 ML) LEMON JUICE

1½ CUPS (188 G) FLOUR

¾ CUP (94 G) WHOLE WHEAT PASTRY FLOUR

2 TABLESPOONS (15 G) COCOA POWDER

2 TEASPOONS BAKING SODA

1 TEASPOON CINNAMON

2 TEASPOONS GROUND GINGER

¼ TEASPOON FRESHLY GRATED NUTMEG

⅛ TEASPOON GROUND CLOVES

¼ TEASPOON SALT

1 CUP (235 ML) DARK BEER

FOR THE FROSTING:

⅓ CUP (67 G) VEGAN SHORTENING

⅓ CUP (75 G) VEGAN MARGARINE

2 CUPS (240 G) POWDERED SUGAR

1 TEASPOON COCOA POWDER

1½ TABLESPOONS (22.5 ML) IRISH WHISKEY

½ TEASPOON VANILLA EXTRACT

GENEROUS ¼ TEASPOON COFFEE EXTRACT

2 TEASPOONS NONDAIRY MILK

Pumpkin Spice Beer Bread

This quick bread is a bit more savory than sweet, and perfect with a mug of hot apple cider. The toasted pumpkin seeds are an optional garnish, but recommended if you are making your own pumpkin purée from winter squash.

YIELD: 1 LOAF

FOR THE PUMPKIN SEEDS:

½ CUP (32 G) RAW PUMPKIN SEEDS

½ TEASPOON SALT

2 TEASPOONS MAPLE SYRUP

1 TEASPOON CANOLA OIL

½ TEASPOON CINNAMON

PINCH OF GROUND CLOVES

PINCH OF FRESHLY GRATED NUTMEG

FRESHLY GROUND BLACK PEPPER, TO
    TASTE

FOR THE BREAD:

3 CUPS (375 G) FLOUR

¼ CUP (50 G) SUGAR

1 TABLESPOON (14 G) BAKING POWDER

¼ TEASPOON SALT

1 TEASPOON CINNAMON

½ TEASPOON GROUND GINGER

¼ TEASPOON GROUND CARDAMOM

⅛ TEASPOON GROUND CLOVES

⅛ TEASPOON FRESHLY GRATED NUTMEG

1 CUP (245 G) PUMPKIN PURÉE

2 TABLESPOONS (30 ML) OIL

1 CUP (235 ML) PUMPKIN BEER

To make the pumpkin seeds: Preheat oven to 350°F (180°C, or gas mark 4).

Combine all the ingredients in a bowl and stir until the seeds are completely coated.

Spread seeds on a baking sheet lined with foil or parchment paper and bake for 20 to 25 minutes, stirring every 5 minutes, until fragrant and crispy.

To make the bread: Prepare an 8 x 4-inch (20.5 x 10 cm) loaf pan with parchment paper or oil.

Combine the flour, sugar, baking powder, salt, and spices in a large mixing bowl. Create a well in the center of dry ingredients and add the pumpkin purée, oil, and beer.

Stir until just combined, then pour the mixture into your loaf pan. If you're using the pumpkin seeds, sprinkle them atop the loaf and press down slightly.

Bake for 55 minutes, or until a toothpick inserted into the center comes out clean and the top is firm.

If you check on the loaf and find the pumpkin seeds are starting to get too crispy, cover the top with foil and continue baking.

Let sit in the pan on a cooling rack for 15 to 20 minutes, then turn out onto a flat surface and let cool a bit longer before slicing. Enjoy with apple butter, coconut spread, or another topping of your choosing.

Malted Beer Float

This adult root beer float is fantastic with a nice stout.

YIELD: 2 SERVINGS

1 TABLESPOON (15 ML) BARLEY MALT
SYRUP

4 SCOOPS CHOCOLATE MALT ICE CREAM
(PAGE 97)

1½ CUPS (355 ML) BEER

Place 2 glasses in the freezer for 15 to 20 minutes. Remove both glasses from the freezer, and drizzle ½ tablespoon (7.5 ml) barley malt syrup in each glass. Put 2 scoops ice cream in each glass, then top them off with ¾ cup (175 ml) beer each.

RECIPE NOTE
If you want to make premade vanilla dairy-free ice cream into malt ice cream, stir 2 tablespoons (30 ml) barley malt syrup into four scoops of ice cream. Stick back in the freezer until ready to make the beer floats.

Beer Soft Pretzels

Bar snacks become a substantial treat when beer is mixed into a warm, fluffy soft pretzel sprinkled with salt. As an alternative, forgo the pretzel shape and make pretzel buns for sandwiches or veggie burgers!

YIELD: 8 TO 10 PRETZELS

¼ CUP (60 ML) WARM WATER

1 PACKAGE (9 G) YEAST

1 TABLESPOON (13 G) SUGAR

1¼ CUPS (295 ML) WARM BEER (A LITTLE LESS THAN A BOTTLE)

2 TABLESPOONS (30 ML) OLIVE OIL

1 TEASPOON SALT

4 CUPS (500 G) FLOUR

½ CUP (110 G) BAKING SODA

OLIVE OIL, FOR BRUSHING

COARSE SALT (PRETZEL SALT), FOR SPRINKLING

Combine the water, yeast, and sugar in a large bowl, or stand mixer affixed with a dough hook, and let sit until bubbly, about 5 minutes.

Add beer, oil, and salt to yeast mixture and stir until combined. Add flour, 1 cup (125 g) at a time, mixing in between additions until a bread-like dough is formed. When the dough forms into a ball and no longer sticks to the sides of the bowl, knead for 8 minutes, either by hand on a floured surface or with the dough hook.

Form the dough into a tight ball and place in an oiled bowl. Cover with plastic wrap or a towel and let rise for 1 hour, or until doubled in size.

Preheat oven to 425°F (220°C, or gas mark 7). Line a cookie sheet with parchment paper. Bring a large pot of water to a boil.

While you're waiting for the water to boil, start forming your pretzels. Divide the dough into 8 to 10 cupcake-sized pieces. Roll each piece of dough into a long rope, at least a foot long, and twist into a pretzel shape. Set on the parchment-lined cookie sheet and repeat until all your pretzels are formed.

When the water is boiling, stir in the baking soda until it dissolves. Boil your pretzels, 2 at a time, for 30 to 40 seconds. They will rise to the top of the water and firm up to retain their shape. Place the pretzels back on the cookie sheet and repeat for all the pretzels.

Once you're done boiling, brush each pretzel with olive oil and sprinkle on a bit of coarse salt. Place the cookie sheet in the oven and bake for 13 to 14 minutes, or until golden brown. Let cool on the sheet, then devour with spicy mustard!

Beeramisu

Because this recipe isn't baked, the ingredients you choose are extremely flexible. If desired, add more coffee than beer, and choose whichever liqueur you have on hand or want to use. If you're craving a more traditional tiramisu, leave out the beer entirely and replace with more coffee or espresso.

YIELD: 12 SERVINGS

½ CUP (120 ML) STRONG BREWED COFFEE OR ESPRESSO

½ CUP (120 ML) DARK BEER

2 TABLESPOONS (30 ML) COFFEE LIQUEUR, AMARETTO, OR HAZELNUT LIQUEUR (OR A MIX)

1½ CUPS (345 G) MASCARPONE (PAGE 169)

½ CUP (120 ML) COCONUT CREAM

1 TABLESPOON (15 ML) AMARETTO OR COFFEE LIQUEUR

½ TEASPOON COFFEE EXTRACT OR 1 TABLESPOON (15 ML) COFFEE LIQUEUR

20 TO 24 LADYFINGERS (OPPOSITE PAGE)

COCOA POWDER OR CHOCOLATE SHAVINGS, FOR TOPPING

Combine the coffee or espresso, beer, and liqueur in a shallow dish. Set aside.

Combine the mascarpone with the coconut cream and whisk until combined. Stir in the amaretto or coffee liqueur, and coffee extract.

Prepare an 8-inch (20.5 cm) square baking pan with cooking spray or margarine.

Dip the ladyfingers in the coffee-beer mixture one at a time, for 3 to 4 seconds, then place them in the bottom of the pan. You don't want to let them soak too long because that will make them mushy; however, if you don't soak them long enough, the cookies will still need moisture and absorb the mascarpone mixture instead. Slice some of the cookies lengthwise to fill gaps between the cookies and the sides of the pan. You should use 10 to 12 ladyfingers total for the first layer.

Once you've finished the first layer, spoon half the mascarpone mixture atop the cookies. Spread it out evenly and make sure no cookie bits are showing.

Repeat the dipping process for another layer of ladyfingers.

Once you've completed two layers, top the whole thing with the rest of the mascarpone mixture. Cover with plastic wrap and chill in the refrigerator for at least 2 hours before serving so the flavors have a chance to meld.

Right before serving, lightly sift cocoa powder on top, or top the tiramisu with chocolate curls.

RECIPE NOTES
- Don't open another can of coconut milk for this recipe! After making the mascarpone, there should be roughly ½ cup (120 ml) coconut cream left to use for this recipe.
- Make chocolate shavings and curls by shaving a chocolate bar with a vegetable peeler in long strokes.

Ladyfingers

These spongy, crisp cookies are a natural in tiramisu or Beeramisu (opposite page), but they can be served with coffee or used in icebox cakes and trifles.

Cream together the margarine, sugar, and agave nectar in a stand mixer or in a bowl with a fork.

Add the yogurt, milk, and vanilla and mix until combined.

Add the baking powder, cream of tartar, and salt. Add flour 1 cup (125 g) at a time, mixing after each addition, until a ball of dough forms.

Refrigerate the dough for 1 hour or up to overnight. Alternatively, you can freeze the dough for about 20 minutes if you're in a hurry.

Preheat oven to 350°F (180°C, or gas mark 4). Take golf ball–sized portions of dough and roll them into logs, a little under 4 inches (10 cm) long. Place on a parchment-lined cookie sheet.

Bake for 12 to 14 minutes, or until golden on the bottoms and soft on top. Cool on a wire rack.

YIELD: 24 LADYFINGERS

⅔ CUP (150 G) VEGAN MARGARINE

1¼ CUPS (250 G) SUGAR

2 TABLESPOONS (30 ML) AGAVE NECTAR

½ CUP (115 G) VANILLA-FLAVORED NON-DAIRY YOGURT

¼ CUP (60 ML) NONDAIRY MILK

½ TEASPOON VANILLA EXTRACT

1 TABLESPOON (14 G) BAKING POWDER

½ TEASPOON CREAM OF TARTAR

¼ TEASPOON SALT

4 CUPS (500 G) FLOUR

Red Wine Chocolate Cupcakes

These chocolate cupcakes are infused with Cabernet and look delicate and fancy with generous swirls of frosting and chocolate curls. The wine in the cupcakes lends a full, fruity flavor to the cocoa, and a blush color in the frosting—the perfect balance of light and dark flavors.

YIELD: 12 CUPCAKES

FOR THE CUPCAKES:
2 CUPS (470 ML) CABERNET SAUVIGNON OR OTHER RED WINE
½ CUP (112 G) VEGAN MARGARINE
¾ CUP (150 G) SUGAR
½ CUP (115 G) PLAIN OR VANILLA-FLAVORED NONDAIRY YOGURT
¼ CUP (60 ML) NONDAIRY MILK
1½ TEASPOONS VANILLA EXTRACT
1 CUP (125 G) FLOUR
½ CUP (59 G) COCOA POWDER
2 TEASPOONS BAKING POWDER
¼ TEASPOON BAKING SODA
¼ TEASPOON SALT

FOR THE FROSTING:
½ CUP (112 G) VEGAN MARGARINE
½ CUP (100 G) VEGAN SHORTENING
3 CUPS (360 G) POWDERED SUGAR
½ TEASPOON VANILLA EXTRACT
1 TABLESPOON (15 ML) NONDAIRY MILK

FOR GARNISH:
VEGAN DARK CHOCOLATE BAR

To make the cupcakes: Pour the wine in a saucepan and bring to a boil. Lower the heat to a high simmer and cook for about 20 minutes, or until the wine reduces nearly to a syrup consistency. Don't let it thicken.

Set the reduction aside. It should be 3 to 4 tablespoons (45 to 60 ml) and will be used in the cupcakes, frosting, and as a drizzle.

Preheat oven to 350°F (180°C, or gas mark 4) and line a cupcake pan with 12 liners. Cream together margarine and sugar.

Add yogurt, 4 teaspoons wine reduction, milk, and vanilla, then mix until incorporated.

In a separate bowl, sift together the flour, cocoa, baking powder, baking soda, and salt.

Add the dry ingredients to the wet ingredients and mix until the batter is smooth. It should be airy but somewhat thick.

Fill each cupcake liner two-thirds full and bake for 18 to 20 minutes or until a toothpick inserted in the center comes out clean. Remove from oven and let cool.

To make the frosting: Cream together margarine and shortening. Gradually add the powdered sugar while mixing.

Add 1 teaspoon wine reduction, vanilla, and milk, then beat until light and fluffy, 5 to 8 minutes. If the frosting is too thick, add another splash of milk.

Fill up your pastry bag and pipe big swirls of frosting on your cupcakes once they've cooled. Drizzle the remaining wine reduction evenly over the cupcakes.

Using a vegetable peeler, peel thick chocolate curls from the chocolate bar. Stick them in the freezer for a few minutes to firm, then garnish each cupcake with curls.

RECIPE NOTE
The wine reduction is used in the cupcake batter, frosting, and as a drizzle, so remember to save some as you go.

Mulled Wine

Mulled wine is a warm, spicy, and soothing fall and wintertime drink to curl up with under some blankets. All the spices and citrus make your house smell amazing while it cooks. I prefer a mulled wine with lots of spices, a hint of citrus, and only a bit of sugar.

YIELD: 1 QUART (940 ML)

3¼ CUPS (750 ML OR 1 BOTTLE) RED WINE

JUICE OF 1 ORANGE (SAVE THE ORANGE
   HALVES)

1 CUP (235 ML) APPLE JUICE OR CIDER

3 CINNAMON STICKS

½ VANILLA BEAN

8 WHOLE CLOVES

4 CARDAMOM PODS

2 WHOLE STAR ANISE

4 WHOLE PEPPERCORNS

PINCH OF FRESHLY GRATED NUTMEG

1 TEASPOON DRIED ROSEBUDS
   OR ROSEWATER

⅓ CUP (80 ML) AGAVE NECTAR (OR
   ½ CUP [100 G] SUGAR)

Combine all the ingredients, including the orange halves, in a large saucepan and turn the heat to medium. Bring almost to a boil, then reduce the heat to a low simmer.

Simmer for 20 minutes, then remove the oranges and ladle the wine into mugs. The flavors mature the longer the spices are in in the wine, so keep them in the saucepan if there are any leftovers, and reheat on the stove as needed.

Rose Rosé Shortbread Cookies

The rosewater shines in these crisp, buttery little cookies topped with a sweet wine glaze. Be sure to use concentrated rosewater to avoid adding excess moisture. Any type of white wine can be used in the glaze, but the rosé lends a lovely touch of color.

YIELD: 30 COOKIES

FOR THE COOKIES:

1 CUP (225 G) VEGAN MARGARINE
¾ CUP (90 G) POWDERED SUGAR
1 TEASPOON ROSEWATER
¼ TEASPOON SALT
2¼ CUPS (281 G) FLOUR

FOR THE GLAZE:

2½ TABLESPOONS (38 ML) ROSÉ OR
   OTHER WHITE WINE
1 CUP (120 ML) POWDERED SUGAR

To make the cookies: Preheat oven to 350°F (180°C, or gas mark 4).

In a large bowl or stand mixer, beat the margarine and powdered sugar together until smooth. Add the rosewater and mix until an even consistency is achieved.

Add the salt, then sift in the flour. Mix well until combined. The dough should be similar to sugar cookie dough, neither sticky nor dry. If it's too soft, chill the bowl in the refrigerator for 10 minutes.

Transfer dough to a gallon-sized resealable plastic bag. Keeping the bag unzipped, use a rolling pin to flatten the dough evenly, making sure to spread it into the bottom corners, then work your way up to the open end. The dough should nearly fill the bag, and should only be about ⅛ inch (0.5 cm) thick.

Refrigerate the rolled-out dough (make sure to keep it flat) for about 30 minutes. When the dough is firm, cut the plastic bag open at the seams and turn the dough onto a cutting board. Using a sharp knife, trim off any uneven edges. Cut the dough into 2-inch (5 cm) squares.

Gently lift each square from the cutting board and place on a parchment-lined cookie sheet. Poke each cookie twice with a fork.

Bake for 9 to 12 minutes, until the edges are golden brown. Immediately transfer to a cooling rack to cool completely.

To make the glaze: In a medium bowl, combine the wine and powdered sugar and stir until smooth. The consistency should be thick, but thin enough to drizzle, neither watery nor paste-like. Add more wine or powdered sugar if necessary.

Drizzle or dollop the glaze on the shortbread, let set, then enjoy.

Red Wine Chocolate Truffles

These truffles are the perfect finish to a dinner party or small gathering.

YIELD: 15 TO 20 TRUFFLES

2 CUPS (350 G) VEGAN CHOCOLATE CHIPS
½ CUP (120ML) RED WINE
2 TABLESPOONS (28 G) NONDAIRY MILK
¼ CUP (56 G) VEGAN MARGARINE
COCOA POWDER, FOR ROLLING

Melt the chocolate, wine, and milk together in a double boiler over medium heat or in a glass bowl in the microwave, then pour into a bowl if necessary. Stir until completely smooth, then set aside for 5 minutes.

Fill another bowl with ice and about 1 cup (235 ml) water.

Place the bowl filled with the melted chocolate into the ice bath. Using electric beaters on high speed, start whipping up the chocolate evenly around the bowl. Add the margarine and continue whipping.

You will see bubbles forming everywhere, and the chocolate mixture will start to thicken up to the consistency of heavy cream after a few minutes. Continue whipping until the consistency becomes very thick, then stop. Over-whipping could cause the filling to become soft and collapse or become grainy.

Place the bowl in the refrigerator and let chill and thicken.

Prepare a baking sheet with parchment paper or a silicone mat and pour some cocoa powder into a shallow bowl.

Using a small cookie scoop, make balls that are about 1 inch (2.5 cm) in diameter, then roll in the cocoa powder and place on the baking sheet.

Place the tray of rolled truffles in the refrigerator for at least 1 hour, then eat! Keep stored in refrigerator in an airtight container for up to 2 weeks.

Mini Red Wine Mousse Cake

This mini cake frosted with pillows of dark chocolate mousse is lovely with Merlot or Cabernet Sauvignon.

YIELD: 6 TO 8 SERVINGS

FOR THE CAKES:

2 CUPS (470 ML) RED WINE

1⅔ CUPS (208 G) FLOUR

½ CUP (59 G) COCOA POWDER

1 CUP (200 G) SUGAR

1¼ TEASPOONS BAKING SODA

¼ TEASPOON SALT

¾ TEASPOON VANILLA EXTRACT

1 TABLESPOON (15 ML) BALSAMIC
   VINEGAR

⅓ CUP (80 ML) CANOLA OIL

½ CUP (120 ML) NONDAIRY MILK

½ CUP (120 ML) SELTZER WATER OR
   GINGER ALE

FOR THE FILLING:

1 HEAPING CUP (178 G) SLICED
   STRAWBERRIES

2 TEASPOONS CORNSTARCH

3 TABLESPOONS (45 ML) AGAVE NECTAR

3 TO 4 TABLESPOONS (45 TO 60 ML)
   RED WINE

2 CUPS (470 ML) CHOCOLATE MOUSSE
   (PAGE 166) MADE WITH RED WINE

To make the cake: Pour wine into a saucepan and bring to a rapid simmer. Let simmer for about 20 minutes, until the wine reduces to ¼ cup (60 ml), which will be one-eighth of the original amount of wine, so you can eyeball it. If you reduce too much, simply reconstitute with water. Set aside to use in the cake.

Preheat oven to 325°F (170°C, or gas mark 3). Line two 6-inch round cake pans with parchment paper.

Sift the flour, cocoa powder, sugar, baking soda, and salt into a bowl or stand mixer.

Create a well in the middle of the dry ingredients and pour in the vanilla, balsamic vinegar, oil, milk, seltzer, and wine reduction. Stir to combine. The batter should be thick but pourable.

Divide the batter evenly between the pans, then bake for 30 to 35 minutes, or until a toothpick inserted in the center comes out clean. Let the cake sit in the pan for 15 to 20 minutes, then remove from the pan and let cool on a wire rack.

To make the filling: Combine strawberries, cornstarch, agave nectar, and 1 tablespoon (15 ml) of the wine in a small saucepan and dissolve the cornstarch.

Turn heat to medium and cook while stirring constantly. As it starts to get thick, add the rest of the wine and cook until it's completely incorporated and thickens up like jam.

When the cakes are cool, spread the strawberry filling on one cake, and top with the other.

Frost cake with mousse and garnish with fresh strawberries. Store in the refrigerator, but remove it shortly before serving so the mousse can soften up.

RECIPE NOTE
Although this recipe makes the perfect amount of batter for a two-layer mini cake (6-inch [15 cm] pans), it is the equivalent to 18 cupcakes. If you prefer cupcakes, bake for 18 minutes at 350°F (180°C, or gas mark 4).

White Raspberry Chardonnay Bundt Cake

This light bundt cake is filled with fresh berries, white chocolate, and white wine. Use any white wine, like Chardonnay, or rosé. Champagne would also be delicious.

YIELD: 12 TO 16 SERVINGS

FOR THE CAKE:

1 CUP (225 G) VEGAN MARGARINE

1¼ CUPS (250 G) SUGAR

¾ CUP (90 G) POWDERED SUGAR

¾ CUP (170 G) BERRY- OR VANILLA-
FLAVORED NONDAIRY YOGURT

⅓ CUP (80 ML) NONDAIRY MILK

½ CUP (120 ML) WHITE WINE

2 TEASPOONS VANILLA EXTRACT

3⅓ CUPS (405 G) FLOUR

1½ TABLESPOONS (21 G) BAKING POWDER

½ TEASPOON SALT

1 CUP (155 G) CHOPPED FRESH
RASPBERRIES

¼ CUP (44 G) VEGAN WHITE CHOCOLATE
CHIPS

FOR THE GANACHE:

¼ CUP (44 G) VEGAN WHITE CHOCOLATE
CHIPS

2 TABLESPOONS (30 ML) WHITE WINE

½ CUP (60 G) POWDERED SUGAR

COCONUT CREAM (PAGE 168) OR OTHER
NONDAIRY WHIPPED CREAM, FOR
TOPPING (OPTIONAL)

To make the cake: Preheat oven to 350°F (180°C, or gas mark 4). Grease the insides of a 12-cup (2820 ml) standard bundt pan with oil or margarine.

Cream together the margarine and sugars until smooth, then add the yogurt, milk, wine, and vanilla extract. Continue mixing until everything is combined.

Reserve 2 tablespoons (15 g) flour. Sift in the rest of the flour, baking powder, and salt and whisk until almost combined.

Toss the raspberries with the reserved flour, then stir into the batter along with the white chocolate chips. The batter should be somewhat thick and fragrant.

Bake for 45 minutes or until the top is firm and a toothpick inserted in the center comes out clean. Transfer to a wire rack to cool. After 30 to 45 minutes, loosen the edges with a knife and turn out the cake. Let the cake finish cooling completely.

To make the ganache: Melt the white chocolate in a double boiler on the stove over medium heat or in a glass bowl in the microwave, then stir in the wine and powdered sugar. Let cool slightly before drizzling onto the cake.

Serve with raspberries or berries and a dollop of whipped cream.

> **RECIPE NOTE**
> The raspberries can be replaced with another fresh fruit, like cherries or strawberries.

Champagne Mousse Petit Fours

Covered in ganache and topped with mousse, these cakes are quite rich.

YIELD: 16 PETIT FOURS

FOR THE CAKES:

2 CUPS (250 G) FLOUR

½ CUP (100 G) SUGAR

½ TEASPOON BAKING POWDER

½ TEASPOON BAKING SODA

¼ TEASPOON SALT

¾ CUP (176 ML) CHAMPAGNE

¼ CUP (60 ML) NONDAIRY MILK

1 TABLESPOON (15 ML) AGAVE NECTAR

⅓ CUP (80 ML) CANOLA OIL

1 TEASPOON VANILLA EXTRACT

FOR THE GANACHE:

2½ CUPS (438 G) VEGAN CHOCOLATE
   CHIPS

⅔ CUP (160 ML) NONDAIRY MILK OR
   CREAMER

FOR THE DRIZZLE:

½ CUP (88 G) VEGAN WHITE CHOCOLATE
   CHIPS

1 TABLESPOON (12.5 G) VEGAN SHORT-
   ENING OR OIL

2 CUPS (470 ML) CHOCOLATE MOUSSE
   (PAGE 166) MADE WITH CHAMPAGNE

To make the cakes: Preheat oven to 350°F (180°C, or gas mark 4). Line an 8-inch (20.5 cm) square baking pan with parchment paper.

Sift together the flour, sugar, baking powder, baking soda, and salt. Make a well in the center of the dry ingredients and pour in the Champagne, milk, agave nectar, oil, and vanilla. Whisk together all the ingredients until combined.

The batter should be thick, much like muffin batter. Pour into prepared pan and bake for 18 to 20 minutes, until the top is golden, the cake is very firm to the touch, and it springs back when touched.

Remove cake from the oven and let cool for 5 to 10 minutes. Loosen the sides with a butter knife, turn the cake out onto a cooling rack, and let cool completely.

Cut the cake into 16 squares. If the edge pieces aren't in perfect squares, feel free to slice off the edges to even them out.

To make the ganache: Melt the chocolate and milk together in a glass bowl in the microwave or in a double boiler over medium heat. Line a cookie sheet with parchment paper and place all cakes on the sheet, spaced apart.

Spoon ganache over each cake. Let set.

To make the drizzle: Melt white chocolate and shortening together in a glass bowl in the microwave or over a double boiler over medium heat.

Pour white chocolate into a pastry bag affixed with a writing tip, or a large zip-top bag with one corner snipped off. Drizzle the white chocolate on each petit four.

Pipe or dollop mousse atop each petit four.

Wine-Poached Pears with Mascarpone

A classic, healthful, and brilliantly colored dessert, poached pears are a real treat.

YIELD: 4 SERVINGS

4 FIRM BUT RIPE PEARS

2½ CUPS (558 ML) RED WINE

⅔ CUP (160 ML) WATER

ZEST OF 1 LEMON

JUICE OF 1 LEMON

2 TABLESPOONS (30 ML) GRAND MARNIER
   OR OTHER ORANGE LIQUEUR

1 CINNAMON STICK

1 STAR ANISE

3 OR 4 WHOLE CLOVES

1 VANILLA BEAN

¼ TEASPOON SALT

MASCARPONE (PAGE 169), FOR SERVING

Peel the pears and slice off the bottoms so the pears easily sit upright.

Combine the rest of the ingredients except for the mascarpone in a medium saucepan and turn the heat to medium high. Bring almost to a boil, stirring frequently to dissolve the sugar, 4 to 5 minutes.

Add the pears, then lower the heat to a low simmer. Poach the pears for 15 to 25 minutes (it will vary based on how ripe the pears are), turning halfway through, until the pears are a deep red color and easily pierced with a fork.

Let the pears cool a bit in the liquid until they can be handled. The longer the pears sit in the liquid, the more color and flavor they will absorb.

Remove the pears from the liquid and let finish cooling on a plate. Wipe off any pieces of lemon zest.

Strain spices and lemon zest out of the liquid, then return to the pan. There should be just about 2 cups (470 ml) of liquid left after poaching. Bring to a low boil and reduce to a syrup, about half the volume. This should take about 20 minutes. Remove from heat and let cool a bit.

Stand the pears upright on dessert plates, drizzle with the syrup, and serve with mascarpone.

REPLACING THE ALCOHOL
Use cranberry or pomegranate juice instead of wine, and a few pinches of orange zest instead of Grand Marnier.

Orange Liqueur Pistachio Cannoli

Although there are infinite cannoli variations, this recipe relies on a wine-flavored cannoli shell with an orange liqueur cream filling and a chocolate and chopped pistachio garnish.

YIELD: 12 TO 14 CANNOLI

FOR THE SHELLS:

2 CUPS (250 G) FLOUR

2 TABLESPOONS (26 G) SUGAR

¼ TEASPOON SALT

¼ CUP (56 G) VEGAN MARGARINE

2 TABLESPOONS (29 G) VEGAN SOUR CREAM

⅓ CUP (80 ML) SWEET MARSALA OR WHITE WINE

1 TEASPOON VANILLA EXTRACT

VEGETABLE OR CANOLA OIL, FOR FRYING

FOR THE GARNISH:

1½ CUPS (263 G) VEGAN SEMISWEET CHOCOLATE CHIPS

1 TABLESPOON (12.5 G) VEGAN SHORTENING OR OIL

⅓ CUP (63 G) COARSELY CHOPPED PISTACHIOS

FOR THE FILLING:

1½ CUPS (345 G) OF MASCARPONE (PAGE 169)

½ CUP (60 G) POWDERED SUGAR

½ TEASPOON VANILLA EXTRACT

1 TEASPOON ORANGE ZEST

1 TABLESPOON (15 ML) GRAND MARNIER OR COFFEE LIQUEUR

PINCH OF CINNAMON

To make the shells: Combine flour, sugar, and salt in a large mixing bowl. Using a pastry cutter or your hands, cut in the margarine and incorporate into the dry ingredients until small pebbles are formed.

Add the sour cream, wine, and vanilla, and mix until a dough forms. If the dough is too dry, add more wine.

On a floured surface, roll the dough paper-thin. Cut out rounds with a 3- to 4-inch (7.5 to 10 cm) cookie cutter. Roll each round into an oval shape.

Take an oval with the long side facing you and place a metal cannoli tube lengthwise at the bottom edge. Roll the dough around the cannoli tube, then pinch and press the seam shut so the tube doesn't unroll while frying. Flare out edges.

Fill a large pot or Dutch oven with 2 to 3 inches (5 to 7.5 cm) of oil and heat to about 375°F (190°C) over medium-high heat. Place a cooling rack over a cookie sheet lined with paper towels or a paper bag to catch oil drips.

Fry 2 or 3 cannoli at a time, seam side down, for about 1 minute on each side, until bubbly and golden. Transfer to cooling rack.

To make the garnish: Melt chocolate and shortening and stir until smooth. Dip both edges of each tube in chocolate and place on a cookie sheet lined with parchment paper.

Sprinkle chopped pistachios on the wet chocolate.

To make the filling: Stir together filling ingredients in a small bowl. Spoon the mixture into a pastry bag or zip-top bag. Pipe the filling into each cannoli. The shells will get soggy, so do this step right before serving.

RECIPE NOTE
Cannoli tubes can be found at kitchen supply stores, Italian groceries, and online.

the cocktail lounge

Break out the fancy for these desserts! Favorite cocktails are re-created in sweet treat form, right down to the tiny umbrella, salt rim, and cherry on top.

Margarita Biscotti

These biscotti are the quintessential cookie representation of a standard margarita, right down to the salt rim. They are a perfect finish to any summer meal.

YIELD: 18 TO 20 BISCOTTI

FOR THE BISCOTTI:

½ CUP (112 G) VEGAN MARGARINE

¾ CUP (150 G) SUGAR

2 TABLESPOONS (30 ML) COCONUT MILK
   (FROM A CARTON, NOT A CAN)

1 TABLESPOON (15 ML) LIME JUICE

1 TEASPOON LIME ZEST

1 TABLESPOON (15 ML) TEQUILA

½ TEASPOON VANILLA EXTRACT

2 CUPS (250 G) FLOUR

1½ TEASPOONS BAKING POWDER

¼ TEASPOON SALT

FOR THE GLAZE:

1½ TABLESPOONS (22.5 ML) LIME JUICE

2 TEASPOONS TEQUILA

¾ CUP (90 G) POWDERED SUGAR

2 TEASPOONS VEGAN MARGARINE

¼ TEASPOON LIME ZEST

SEA SALT, FOR GARNISH

To make the biscotti: Preheat oven to 325°F (170°C, or gas mark 3).

Cream together the margarine, sugar, coconut milk, lime juice, zest, tequila, and vanilla extract with an electric mixer. Add in the flour, baking powder, and salt.

Form dough into a 3-inch (7.5 cm) wide and 1-inch (2.5 cm) thick loaf and bake on a parchment-lined or lightly greased cookie sheet for about 30 minutes.

Let cool for 10 to 15 minutes, then slice into ½-inch (1 cm) wedges and bake for 5 more minutes on each side. Remove from the oven and let cool.

To make the glaze: Combine all the glaze ingredients except the salt in a small bowl and stir until smooth. Drizzle glaze on cooled biscotti and let sit for 5 to 10 minutes. Sprinkle salt atop each biscotti, then let the glaze set completely.

Tequila Sunrise Ice Cream

The hues and flavors of a tequila sunrise translate beautifully in this sweet coconut-based ice cream. The agave-sweetened orange ice cream is glazed with a potent tequila grenadine syrup, mimicking the visual sunrise element of the drink. Don't forget the cherry and orange slice garnish!

YIELD: 1½ PINTS (428 G)

FOR THE ICE CREAM:

2 CANS (15 OUNCES OR 440 ML EACH) COCONUT MILK

⅔ CUP (160 ML) AGAVE NECTAR

1 TABLESPOON (6 G) FINELY GRATED ORANGE ZEST

2 TABLESPOONS (30 ML) TEQUILA

¼ CUP (60 ML) ORANGE JUICE

1 TEASPOON ORANGE EXTRACT

2 TABLESPOONS (30 ML) GRENADINE

FOR THE SYRUP:

¾ CUP (177 ML) GRENADINE

¼ CUP PLUS 3 TABLESPOONS (105 ML) TEQUILA, DIVIDED

FOR GARNISH:

ORANGE SLICES

MARASCHINO CHERRIES

To make the ice cream: Let one of the cans of coconut milk sit undisturbed at room temperature for at least 24 hours, then let chill in the refrigerator for another 24 hours. This will make the cream rise to the top.

Remove the can from the refrigerator and scoop out the cream, discarding the coconut water left behind. Place the cream in a mixing bowl and whisk until soft and smooth.

Add the remaining ingredients, including the other can of coconut milk. Stir until completely combined.

Freeze in an ice cream maker according to manufacturer's instructions. Due to the alcohol content, the ice cream may be a little softer than traditional ice cream.

To make the syrup: Pour the grenadine into a saucepan and bring to a boil over medium-high heat. Lower the heat and simmer for 7 to 8 minutes.

Add the ¼ cup (60 ml) tequila 3 to 4 minutes into the simmering time and continue simmering until the mixture is somewhat thick and syrupy.

Remove from heat and let cool, then stir in the 3 tablespoons (45 ml) tequila (or more, to taste).

To serve, scoop the ice cream onto a plate or into a bowl. Drizzle with grenadine sauce, then garnish with skewered orange slices and maraschino cherries.

Strawberry Amaretto Cake

The rich, nutty, and sweet flavor of amaretto complements bright strawberries in this cake.

YIELD: 12 SERVINGS

FOR THE CAKE:

1 CUP (225 G) VEGAN MARGARINE

1 CUP (200 G) SUGAR

⅔ CUP (80 G) POWDERED SUGAR

½ CUP (115 ML) STRAWBERRY- OR
   VANILLA-FLAVORED NONDAIRY YOGURT

⅔ CUP (160 ML) NONDAIRY MILK

1 TEASPOON LEMON ZEST

3 TABLESPOONS (45 ML) AMARETTO

1 TEASPOON ALMOND EXTRACT

2 TEASPOONS VANILLA EXTRACT

3 CUPS (375 G) FLOUR

4 TEASPOONS BAKING POWDER

½ TEASPOON SALT

FOR THE FILLING:

¾ CUP (128 G) SLICED STRAWBERRIES

2 TEASPOONS CORNSTARCH

1 TABLESPOON (13 G) SUGAR

FOR GARNISH:

AMARETTO BUTTERCREAM (PAGE 168)

FRESH STRAWBERRIES

TOASTED ALMOND SLICES

To make the cake: Preheat oven to 350°F (180°C, or gas mark 4). Line two 8-inch (20.5 cm) square cake pans with parchment and grease the sides of the pan with oil or margarine.

Cream together the margarine and sugars until smooth, then add the yogurt, milk, lemon zest, amaretto, almond extract, and vanilla extract. Continue mixing until everything is combined.

Sift in the flour, baking powder, and salt and whisk until just combined. The batter should be somewhat thick and fragrant. Bake for 30 to 35 minutes or until the tops are firm and a toothpick inserted in the center comes out clean. Transfer to a wire rack to cool. After 10 to 15 minutes, loosen the edges with a knife and turn out the cake pans. Let the cakes finish cooling completely.

To make the filling: Combine sliced strawberries, cornstarch, and sugar in a small saucepan. Stir until cornstarch dissolves into the strawberries and the sugar coats them.

Turn the heat to medium and stir until the sugar dissolves and the cornstarch turns the strawberry juice into a thick syrup, 4 to 5 minutes. Don't overcook the strawberries.

Spread the strawberry filling atop one of the cakes, then place the other cake on top.

Frost the top and sides of the cake with the Amaretto Buttercream, then transfer any remaining frosting to a pastry bag and swirl around the edges.

Garnish with fresh strawberries and toasted almond slices.

Gin-and-Tonic Cranberry Lime Cookies

This moderately sweet cookie teeming with tart lime and gin-soaked cranberries is a great finale for a sophisticated meal.

YIELD: 24 COOKIES

FOR THE COOKIES:
¾ CUP (90 G) DRIED CRANBERRIES
¼ CUP (60 ML) GIN
1 TABLESPOON (15 ML) TONIC WATER
⅔ CUP (150 G) VEGAN MARGARINE
1½ CUPS (180 G) POWDERED SUGAR
½ TEASPOON VANILLA EXTRACT
1 TABLESPOON (15 ML) LIME JUICE
½ TEASPOON LIME ZEST
⅛ TEASPOON SALT
2 CUPS (250 G) FLOUR

FOR THE GLAZE:
UP TO 2 TABLESPOONS (30 ML) GIN
½ CUP (60 G) POWDERED SUGAR
1 TEASPOON LIME JUICE
EXTRA POWDERED SUGAR, FOR
    SPRINKLING

To make the cookies: Coarsely chop the dried cranberries and place in a bowl or glass container. Pour the gin and tonic over the cranberries and let sit for at least 4 hours, stirring occasionally, until the cranberries absorb most of the liquid. Drain the cranberries, reserving any leftover liquid.

Preheat oven to 375°F (190°C, or gas mark 5).

Cream together the margarine and powdered sugar with electric beaters in a medium-large bowl. Add the vanilla, lime juice, zest, and salt.

Gradually sift in the flour, stirring after each addition, then add the gin-soaked cranberries and incorporate them into the mixture.

Roll into 1-inch (2.5 cm) balls, place on a parchment-lined cookie sheet, and bake for 12 minutes.

To make the glaze: Measure out the leftover liquid from the cranberries, and if it's less than 2 tablespoons (30 ml), replenish it with more gin. Stir in the powdered sugar and lime juice. When the cookies are cooled, drizzle the glaze on the cookies. Sprinkle powdered sugar over the glaze.

Coconut White Russian Cupcakes

Coconut milk makes the cupcake version of this rich cocktail even more decadent. These are a breeze to whip up and a perfect treat any time of day.

YIELD: 12 CUPCAKES

FOR THE CUPCAKES:
½ CUP (112 G) VEGAN MARGARINE
½ CUP (100 G) SUGAR
¼ CUP (60 G) BROWN SUGAR
1 TEASPOON GROUND COFFEE BEANS
⅓ CUP (77 G) PLAIN OR VANILLA-
    FLAVORED NONDAIRY YOGURT
½ CUP (120 ML) CANNED COCONUT MILK
2 TABLESPOONS (30 ML) KAHLÚA OR 1
    TO 2 TEASPOONS (5 TO 10 ML) COFFEE
    EXTRACT
⅓ CUP (40 G) POWDERED SUGAR
2 TEASPOONS VANILLA EXTRACT
¼ TEASPOON COCONUT EXTRACT
1½ CUPS (188 G) FLOUR
2 TEASPOONS BAKING POWDER
½ TEASPOON SALT

FOR THE TOPPING:
COFFEE BUTTERCREAM (PAGE 168)
CHOPPED NUTS
TOASTED COCONUT FLAKES

Preheat oven to 350°F (180°C, or gas mark 4). Line a cupcake pan with 12 liners.

Combine margarine, sugar, brown sugar, and coffee in a mixing bowl and cream together with electric beaters.

Add yogurt, coconut milk, Kahlúa, powdered sugar, and vanilla and coconut extracts. Continue beating until fluffy.

Sift in the flour, baking powder, and salt and continue mixing until just combined.

Fill each cupcake liner two-thirds full. Bake for 18 minutes or until cupcakes are firm in the center.

Frost the cooled cupcakes with Coffee Buttercream using either a knife or a pastry bag. Sprinkle each cupcake with nuts or toasted coconut flakes, if desired.

Whiskey Sour Cupcakes

Serve me a sweet one! These lemon cupcakes are topped with a whiskey lemon buttercream and garnished with sugar, Meyer lemon slices, and a maraschino cherry.

YIELD: 12 CUPCAKES

FOR THE CUPCAKES:

½ CUP (112 G) VEGAN MARGARINE

⅔ CUP (133 G) SUGAR

⅓ CUP (40 G) POWDERED SUGAR

½ CUP (115 G) PLAIN NONDAIRY YOGURT

⅓ CUP (80 ML) COCONUT MILK (FROM A CARTON, NOT A CAN)

1 TABLESPOON (6 G) LEMON ZEST

1 TABLESPOON (15 ML) LEMON JUICE

1 TABLESPOON (15 ML) WHISKEY OR BOURBON

1 TEASPOON VANILLA EXTRACT

1½ CUPS (188 G) FLOUR

2 TEASPOONS BAKING POWDER

¼ TEASPOON SALT

FOR THE FROSTING:

⅓ CUP (67 G) VEGAN SHORTENING

⅓ CUP (75 G) VEGAN MARGARINE

2½ CUPS (300 G) POWDERED SUGAR

3 TABLESPOONS (45 ML) WHISKEY OR BOURBON

1 TEASPOON LEMON JUICE

FOR GARNISH:

COARSE SUGAR

MEYER LEMON SLICES

MARASCHINO CHERRIES

To make the cupcakes: Preheat oven to 350°F (180°C, or gas mark 4), and line a cupcake pan with 12 liners.

Cream together the margarine and sugars until smooth, then add the yogurt, coconut milk, lemon zest and juice, whiskey, and vanilla extract. Continue mixing until everything is combined.

Sift in the flour, baking powder, and salt and whisk until just combined. The batter should be somewhat thick and fragrant.

Fill cupcake liners two-thirds full. Bake for 18 minutes or until the tops are firm and a toothpick inserted in the center comes out clean. Transfer to a wire rack to cool.

To make the frosting: In a large bowl or stand mixer, mix shortening and margarine. Gradually add the powdered sugar. When almost all the sugar is incorporated, add the whiskey and lemon juice. Continue beating until completely smooth and fluffy, 8 to 10 minutes.

Spoon frosting into a pastry bag and pipe swirls atop your cupcakes. Sprinkle with sugar, garnish with a lemon slice, and finish with a cherry on top!

RECIPE NOTE

If you can't find coconut yogurt or a Meyer lemon, you can substitute plain soy yogurt and a regular lemon.

Piña Colada Tres Leches Cake

Tres leches, literally translated as "three milks," is a sweet, moist sponge cake traditionally served in Latin countries. *Tres leches* refers to the three dairy products the cake is soaked in—sweetened condensed milk, evaporated milk, and heavy cream. Not to be confused with coconut milk, cream of coconut is sweetened and contains thickening agents.

YIELD: 12 SERVINGS

FOR THE CAKE:

2 CUPS (250 G) FLOUR

½ CUP (100 G) SUGAR

2 TEASPOONS BAKING POWDER

½ TEASPOON BAKING SODA

¼ TEASPOON SALT

1 CUP (235 ML) COCONUT MILK (FROM A CARTON, NOT A CAN)

2 TEASPOONS APPLE CIDER VINEGAR

1 TABLESPOON (15 ML) AGAVE NECTAR

1 TABLESPOON (15 ML) PINEAPPLE JUICE

⅓ CUP (80 ML) CANOLA OIL, MELTED COCONUT OIL, OR A MIX OF THE TWO

1 TEASPOON VANILLA EXTRACT

FOR THE SYRUP AND TOPPING:

⅔ CUP (160 ML) CREAM OF COCONUT

½ CUP (120 ML) CANNED COCONUT MILK

3 TABLESPOONS (45 ML) COCONUT MILK (FROM A CARTON, NOT A CAN)

⅓ CUP (80 ML) PINEAPPLE JUICE

1 TO 2 TABLESPOONS (15 TO 30 ML) RUM (OPTIONAL)

1 CUP (155 G) DICED FRESH OR CANNED PINEAPPLE

COCONUT WHIPPED CREAM (PAGE 167)

To make the cake: Preheat oven to 350°F (180°C, or gas mark 4) and prepare an 8-inch (20.5 cm) square baking pan.

Sift together flour, sugar, baking powder, baking soda, and salt. In a separate bowl, mix coconut milk and apple cider vinegar and let sit for several minutes to curdle.

Make a well in the center of the dry ingredients and pour in the curdled milk, agave nectar, pineapple juice, oil, and vanilla. Whisk together ingredients until combined. The batter should be thick, like muffin batter.

Pour into baking pan and bake for 30 to 32 minutes, until the top is golden and the cake is very firm. Let cool in pan.

To make the syrup and topping: Stir together the cream of coconut, coconut milks, pineapple juice, and rum.

Poke holes everywhere in the cake with a fork. Pour syrup over the cake, letting it sink in before continuing. You want it to soak the cake evenly. Place the cake in the refrigerator for 1 hour.

Remove the cake from the fridge and spread the pineapple chunks on top.

Dollop Coconut Whipped Cream on the cake. Keep refrigerated until it's time to serve. Cut into slices and serve with a maraschino cherry, some pineapple slices, and perhaps even a paper umbrella on top.

RECIPE NOTES
- Pour the syrup over the cake 3 to 4 hours before serving for best results.
- To make a regular *tres leches* cake, omit the pineapples on top of the cake and replace the pineapple juice in the cake with more coconut milk or another nondairy milk.

Blackberry Cosmopolitan Cake

Zesty citrus meets succulent blackberries for a chic cake in a small package. Orange flower water can be found in the ethnic section of the grocery store or in Indian markets.

YIELD: 6 TO 8 SERVINGS

FOR THE CAKE:

¾ CUP (168 G) VEGAN MARGARINE

¾ CUP (150 G) SUGAR

½ CUP (60 G) POWDERED SUGAR

¾ CUP (170 G) BERRY- OR VANILLA-
FLAVORED NONDAIRY YOGURT

½ CUP (120 ML) NONDAIRY MILK

1½ TEASPOONS LIME ZEST

1 TABLESPOON (15 ML) LIME JUICE

1 TEASPOON ORANGE FLOWER WATER

1½ TEASPOONS VANILLA EXTRACT

2¼ CUPS (281 G) FLOUR

1 TABLESPOON (14 G) BAKING POWDER

¼ TEASPOON SALT

⅓ CUP (107 G) BLACKBERRY JAM,
PREFERABLY SEEDLESS

FOR THE FROSTING:

⅓ CUP (75 G) VEGAN MARGARINE

⅓ CUP (67 G) VEGAN SHORTENING

2 CUPS (240 G) POWDERED SUGAR

1 TABLESPOON (15 ML) TRIPLE SEC,
ORANGE LIQUEUR, OR ORANGE JUICE

½ TEASPOON ORANGE ZEST

¼ TEASPOON LIME ZEST

FRESH BLACKBERRIES

ORANGE SLICES

To make the cake: Preheat oven to 350°F (180°C, or gas mark 4). Line two 6-inch (15 cm) round cake pans with parchment circles and grease the sides of the pan with oil or margarine.

Cream together the margarine and sugars until smooth, then add the yogurt, milk, lime zest and juice, orange flower water, and vanilla extract. Continue mixing until everything is combined.

Sift in the flour, baking powder, and salt and whisk until just combined. The batter should be somewhat thick and fragrant.

Fill each cake pan halfway full, then swirl half the blackberry jam in each of the pans. Don't swirl the jam too deeply into the batter because the jam may sink to the bottom.

Bake for 30 to 35 minutes or until the tops are firm and a toothpick inserted in the center comes out clean. Transfer to a wire rack to cool. After 10 to 15 minutes, loosen the edges with a knife and turn out the cakes. Let the cakes finish cooling completely.

Spread the remaining half of the blackberry jam atop one of the cakes, then place the other layer on top.

To make the frosting: Combine margarine and shortening in a large bowl or stand mixer and mix together. Gradually add the powdered sugar. When almost all the sugar is incorporated, add the triple sec, orange zest, and lime zest. Continue beating until completely smooth and fluffy, 8 to 10 minutes.

Frost the top and sides of the cake, then transfer any remaining frosting to a pastry bag and swirl around the edges. Garnish with fresh blackberries and orange slices.

Bananas Foster à la Mode

Looking for an extremely impressive dessert that requires minimal effort? Bananas Foster is the way to go! Lighting your pan on fire is automatically fancy, and everyone around you will forget they had to wait five whole minutes for you to whip up this dessert. I grew up eating bananas Foster, and this is a simple, no-frills recipe.

YIELD: 2 OR 3 SERVINGS

3 TABLESPOONS (52 G) VEGAN
   MARGARINE
½ TEASPOON CINNAMON
½ CUP (115 G) DARK BROWN SUGAR
1 TABLESPOON (15 ML) BANANA LIQUEUR
   OR RUM
3 UNDERRIPE BANANAS, SLICED IN HALF
   LENGTHWISE
¼ CUP (60 ML) DARK RUM
½ TEASPOON VANILLA EXTRACT
VANILLA BEAN ICE CREAM (PAGE 169),
   FOR SERVING

Melt the margarine in a sauté pan over medium heat.

Stir in the cinnamon, brown sugar, and banana liqueur. Stir until the brown sugar dissolves and bubbles, 1 to 2 minutes.

Add the bananas to the pan, stirring and coating them with the syrup, just for a minute. Remove the bananas from the pan and place them on a serving dish.

Add the rum to the syrup left in the pan and quickly stir it in. Using a stick lighter, set the rum in the pan on fire and shake the pan until the flame burns out, 1 to 2 minutes. Remove from heat, and stir in the vanilla.

Serve with dairy-free ice cream. Top the ice cream with the bananas, and pour some syrup from the pan on top. Serve immediately.

RECIPE NOTE
Because we're setting the pan on fire, for the love of boozy bananas, do not use a nonstick pan. Nothing says, "I'm trying to murder you" quite like Bananas Foster à la liquefied Teflon. Using a larger pan is also safer and easier so the flame is evenly distributed.

Caramel Amaretto Apricots with Toasted Almonds

When you can't bring yourself to eat another cookie, or cupcakes are getting you down, a fruit-based dessert is simple and sophisticated.

YIELD: 3 TO 6 SERVINGS

1 TABLESPOON (14 G) VEGAN MARGARINE

3 TABLESPOONS (45 G) BROWN SUGAR

¼ TEASPOON CINNAMON

¼ CUP (60 ML) AMARETTO

3 APRICOTS, HALVED

½ TEASPOON VANILLA EXTRACT

VANILLA BEAN ICE CREAM (PAGE 169), FOR SERVING

3 TABLESPOONS (21 G) CHOPPED ROASTED ALMONDS

Heat a sauté pan to medium-high heat and melt the margarine in the pan.

Whisk in the brown sugar, cinnamon, and 1 tablespoon (15 ml) of the amaretto. Stir until the brown sugar starts to dissolve. Add an additional tablespoon of the amaretto if it's too dry or clumpy.

Reduce the heat to low and place the apricots in the pan, cut side down, and saturate them with the sugar mixture. Cook for 4 minutes on each side, swirling them around occasionally.

If the mixture looks too dry or starts to become thick or crystallize, add a splash of amaretto to deglaze the pan. Continue cooking the apricots until soft and a bit caramelized.

Add the rest of the amaretto to the pan, increase the heat to medium high again, and bring to a light boil. Stirring frequently, boil for 2 minutes or until thick and caramelized.

To serve, drizzle some caramel on a dessert plate, then place an apricot half or two in the center, cut side facing up. Spoon a bit of caramel atop the apricots, then top with a small scoop of ice cream. Drizzle more caramel on the ice cream, and garnish with a sprinkle of chopped roasted almonds.

Absinthe Shortbread Cookies

Modern-day absinthe consumption hearkens to 19th- and 20th-century Europe, where the drink became wildly popular, notably among writers and artists. To serve, a slotted spoon with a single sugar cube is placed on top of a glass containing the bright green liquid. Ice water is slowly dripped into the glass, dissolving the sugar cube, diluting the spirit, and creating a chemical reaction that turns the absinthe a milky green color. Wormwood is one of the three main ingredients of absinthe, but might be difficult to track down and prepare for baking, so two of the three ingredients of "the holy trinity" of absinthe will have to do.

YIELD: 24 COOKIES

¾ CUP (168 G) VEGAN MARGARINE
⅔ CUP (80 G) POWDERED SUGAR
¼ TEASPOON VANILLA EXTRACT
LIME GREEN FOOD COLORING
3 WHOLE STAR ANISE
¼ TEASPOON SALT
1 TABLESPOON (2.5 G) FINELY CHOPPED
  FRESH FENNEL LEAVES
1¾ CUPS (219 G) FLOUR

In a large bowl, beat the margarine and powdered sugar together.

Add the vanilla and food coloring (the amount will vary depending on the intensity of your food coloring). Start with 4 to 5 drops of liquid or a pea-sized amount of gel color and mix thoroughly.

Crush the star anise with a spice grinder or mortar and pestle. Remove any large pieces that wouldn't break up so no one bites into them.

Add the salt, anise, and fennel leaves, then gradually mix in the flour, stirring after each addition until a dough forms. It should be soft, but not wet and sticky. Gradually add additional flour if necessary to reach the right consistency.

Remove the dough from the bowl and roll into a log 2 inches (5 cm) in diameter. Wrap with parchment paper and chill in the refrigerator for at least 1 hour.

Preheat oven to 350°F (180°C, or gas mark 4).

Unroll the parchment paper and cut the dough into ½-inch (1 cm) slices. Line a cookie sheet with the parchment paper, then place the slices on the sheet. Flatten slightly. Bake for 11 to 12 minutes.

Long Island Iced Tea Doughnuts

A lemony cake doughnut infused with citrus and rum flavor topped with a cola-based glaze! Who could ask for more?

YIELD: 10 TO 12 DOUGHNUTS

FOR THE DOUGHNUTS:

2 TABLESPOONS (28 G) VEGAN MARGARINE

2 TABLESPOONS (25 G) VEGAN SHORTENING

¾ CUP (150 G) SUGAR

⅓ CUP (77 G) VANILLA- OR LEMON-FLAVORED NONDAIRY YOGURT

¼ CUP (60 ML) NONDAIRY MILK

2 TABLESPOONS (30 ML) AGAVE NECTAR

1 TABLESPOON (6 G) LEMON ZEST

2 TEASPOONS LIME ZEST

3 TABLESPOONS (45 ML) LEMON JUICE

1 TABLESPOON (15 ML) LIME JUICE

2 TABLESPOONS (30 ML) TRIPLE SEC OR ORANGE JUICE

1 TABLESPOON (15 ML) GIN

1 TEASPOON RUM EXTRACT

3¾ CUPS (506 G) FLOUR

1 TABLESPOON (14 G) BAKING POWDER

½ TEASPOON BAKING SODA

½ TEASPOON SALT

VEGETABLE OIL, FOR FRYING

FOR THE GLAZE:

1¼ TEASPOONS COLA EXTRACT

1½ TABLESPOONS (22.5 ML) RUM

2½ TABLESPOONS (37.5 ML) GIN

1½ CUPS (180 G) POWDERED SUGAR

To make the doughnuts: Cream together margarine and shortening with the sugar. Add the yogurt, milk, agave nectar, lemon and lime zest, lemon and lime juice, triple sec, gin, and rum extract and stir until combined.

In a medium bowl, combine dry ingredients. Add dry ingredients to wet ingredients gradually, stirring after each addition, until a dough forms. The doughnut batter should be dense but airy. If it's sticky or wet, add more flour, because sticky doughnut dough is difficult to work with.

Roll dough into a ball and separate in half. Wrap each portion of the dough in plastic wrap or parchment paper and refrigerate for at least 2 hours, or until firm like sugar cookie dough.

Take one portion of dough and roll it ½ inch (1 cm) thick on a floured surface. Cut rounds using a cookie cutter with a 3-inch (7.5 cm) diameter. Using a small cookie cutter or bottle cap, cut 1-inch (2.5 cm) holes out of the centers of each doughnut.

Take all the dough scraps and repeat to make more doughnuts, then repeat with the other portion of the dough.

Heat at least 2 to 3 inches (5 to 8 cm) of vegetable oil to 375°F (190°C) in a large, heavy-bottomed pot. Place a cooling rack on top of a cookie sheet lined with paper towels to catch oil drips.

Fry 2 or 3 doughnuts at a time for 3 to 4 minutes, turning halfway through, until they are golden on both sides. Place on cooling rack. If they seem to be browning far too rapidly or start to burn, reduce heat.

To make the glaze: Combine cola extract, rum, and gin in a small bowl. Stir in the powdered sugar. The glaze should be pourable, but not liquid or pasty.

Adjust the flavors of the glaze to your tastes. Drizzle the glaze on the finished doughnuts.

Grand Marnier Petit Fours

Inspired by the flavors of French cuisine, here marzipan, Grand Marnier, and dark chocolate are encased within sweet petit fours.

YIELD: 16 PETIT FOURS

FOR THE PETIT FOURS:
2 CUPS (250 G) FLOUR
½ CUP (59 G) COCOA POWDER
1 CUP (200 G) SUGAR
1½ TEASPOONS BAKING SODA
½ TEASPOON SALT
½ CUP (120 ML) CANOLA OIL
1 CUP (235 ML) NONDAIRY MILK
¼ CUP (60 ML) GRAND MARNIER
⅓ CUP (80 ML) ORANGE JUICE
2½ TEASPOONS ORANGE ZEST
1 TEASPOON VANILLA EXTRACT
¼ TEASPOON ALMOND EXTRACT
1 TEASPOON APPLE CIDER VINEGAR
GRAND MARNIER, FOR BRUSHING
⅔ CUP (153 G) MARZIPAN

FOR THE GANACHE:
2½ CUPS (438 G) VEGAN CHOCOLATE
    CHIPS
⅔ CUP (160 ML) NONDAIRY MILK OR
    CREAMER

FOR GARNISH:
ORANGE PEEL
TOASTED ALMONDS
MARZIPAN

To make the petit fours: Preheat oven to 350°F (180°C, or gas mark 4).

Line an 8-inch (20.5 cm) square baking pan with parchment paper, and grease the exposed sides with cooking spray or vegetable oil. Set aside.

Combine the flour, cocoa powder, sugar, baking soda, and salt in a stand mixer or mixing bowl. Stir until combined.

Create a well in the center of the dry ingredients and add the canola oil, milk, Grand Marnier, orange juice and zest, vanilla extract, almond extract, and apple cider vinegar. Mix until just combined.

Pour into the pan and bake for 20 to 22 minutes, until the top is firm and a toothpick inserted in the center comes out clean. Transfer to a wire rack to cool.

When the cake is cool, remove from pan, cut off the edges to even out each side, then cut the square into 16 equal pieces. Slice each piece widthwise through the center, creating 2 layers. Brush both halves with Grand Marnier. Take about 2 teaspoons of marzipan and flatten it out into a square similar in size to a cake piece. Sandwich the marzipan between the cake halves. Repeat with remaining cakes, then brush the top of each cake with more Grand Marnier.

To make the ganache: Melt the chocolate and milk together in a glass bowl in the microwave or on the stovetop in a double boiler over medium heat.

Place cakes on a parchment-lined cookie sheet. Spoon ganache over each cake, spreading it around the sides. Let the chocolate set.

Garnish with orange peel and toasted almonds, or sculpt marzipan balls or fruits.

CHAPTER 9

the cherry on top

These are the recipes that bring everything together and add the essential finishing touch. Make your own mousses, frostings, syrups, and creams.

Chocolate Mousse

This mousse contains no nuts, tofu, agar, added sugar, coconut milk, egg replacer, margarine, or shortening. It's also gluten-free, unaffected by alcohol, and it holds up at room temperature. So, what IS in it? There are only two ingredients: chocolate and your liquid of choice. This is technically called a chocolate chantilly and is really a technique more than a recipe. This is a great alternative to buttercream. It's light and fluffy and can be used to pipe on cupcakes, frost cake, fill pastry, or serve on its own.

YIELD: 2 CUPS (470 ML) MOUSSE

1⅓ CUPS (233 G) CHOCOLATE CHIPS OR CHOPPED CHOCOLATE BAR
1 CUP (235 ML) WATER, TEA, COFFEE, WINE, NONDAIRY MILK, JUICE, DILUTED LIQUOR, OR ANOTHER LIQUID OF YOUR CHOICE

Melt the chocolate and liquid together in a double boiler over medium heat or in a glass bowl in the microwave, then pour into a bowl if necessary. Stir until completely smooth, then set aside.

Fill another bowl up with ice and 1 cup (235 ml) water.

Place the bowl filled with the melted chocolate into the ice bath. Using electric beaters on high speed, start whipping up the chocolate evenly around the bowl. You will see bubbles forming everywhere, and the chocolate mixture will start to thicken up to the consistency of heavy cream after a few minutes.

Stop whipping and stick the bowl in the freezer for a couple minutes. Remove, then continue whipping until thick, then stop. Over-whipping could cause the mousse to become soft and collapse. If that happens, melt the chocolate mixture again and start over (so flexible!).

Let it sit for a few minutes to firm up more before filling a pastry bag or frosting a cake. The mousse gets thicker as it sits untouched, so 5 to 10 minutes is ideal.

RECIPE NOTES
- The ratio is 4 parts chocolate to 3 parts water, so this can be scaled to the desired amount. Smaller batches are easier to work with.
- This recipe will not work with white chocolate.

VARIATIONS:
- Coffee
- Wine
- Grand Marnier
- Tea
- Diluted rosewater
- 2 teaspoons (6 g) culinary lavender steeped in white wine

Coconut Cream

This technique yields thick, luscious coconut cream for use in a myriad of recipes, or it can be whipped up into whipped cream. I like to keep a can of coconut milk in the refrigerator at all times specifically for this purpose. Double, triple, or quadruple this recipe if you need large quantities of whipped cream.

YIELD: 1 CUP (235 ML) COCONUT CREAM

1 CAN (15 OUNCES OR 440 ML) FULL-FAT COCONUT MILK

Let the can of coconut milk sit undisturbed at room temperature for 24 to 48 hours. Then stick it in the fridge at least overnight.

The cream of the coconut milk will have risen to the top of the can and solidified. After chilling, it should have the consistency of solid margarine. If it's mushy, it'll be more like thick heavy cream than fluffy whipped cream and may need to be chilled in the fridge until the last minute before serving.

Scoop out all of the solid cream. You'll be left with coconut water. Retrieve any large chunks of cream from the water, but don't worry about the little chunks floating around. They'll add too much extra moisture to your cream, which is what this whole process is trying to avoid. Discard this water or use it in place of soy milk in a muffin or cake recipe for a hint of coconut flavor.

After you've scooped out all of the cream, you'll have about 1 cup (235 ml). At this point, you can use as directed in a recipe or make Coconut Whipped Cream.

RECIPE NOTE
Coconut Whipped Cream: Whip up the coconut cream with a strong fork, with a hand mixer, or in a stand mixer. Add ¼ cup (30 g) powdered sugar and ½ teaspoon vanilla extract for a touch of sweetness and vanilla flavor. Chill in the fridge until ready to serve, and whip it up before serving.

Basil Simple Syrup

This syrup finds a home in cupcakes and sorbet within this book, but would be a wonderful addition to tea or lemonade.

YIELD: ¾ CUP (180 ML) SYRUP

½ CUP (20 G) LOOSELY PACKED FRESH BASIL
½ CUP (100 G) SUGAR
⅔ CUP (160 ML) WATER

RECIPE NOTE
For Mint Simple Syrup, replace the basil with ½ cup (20 g) fresh mint leaves.

Stack the fresh basil leaves atop each other, roll the stack up tightly, then slice the roll finely to produce thin ribbons. This is called chiffonade and will allow the herbs to infuse the syrup with the most flavor.

Combine the sugar and water in a saucepan over medium-high heat and bring to a boil, stirring constantly. Continue to stir and boil until all the sugar is dissolved and the mixture is clear.

Remove from heat and stir in the herbs. Completely submerge the leaves and coat thoroughly with the syrup. Herbs like basil lose their flavor at high temperatures, so don't be tempted to put the saucepan back on the heat. Let the basil sit in the syrup for 45 minutes to 1 hour. Strain basil leaves from the syrup using cheesecloth or a fine metal strainer and discard.

Basic Buttercream

This recipe is for straight-up vanilla buttercream for all your frosting needs! The flavors can be altered as you like.

YIELD: 1½ CUPS (346 G), OR ENOUGH TO FROST 12 CUPCAKES

⅓ CUP (75 G) VEGAN MARGARINE
⅓ CUP (67 G) VEGAN SHORTENING
2½ CUPS (280 G) POWDERED SUGAR
1 TEASPOON VANILLA EXTRACT
1 TO 2 TABLESPOONS (15 TO 30 ML) NON-DAIRY MILK

Combine the margarine and shortening in a large bowl or stand mixer and mix together.

Gradually add the powdered sugar. When almost all the sugar is incorporated, add the vanilla and milk.

Continue beating until completely smooth and fluffy, 8 to 10 minutes.

RECIPE NOTES
- Cherry Buttercream: Omit milk and vanilla and add 1 tablespoon (15 ml) grenadine and 1½ tablespoons (23 ml) maraschino cherry juice.
- Butterscotch Buttercream: Add ½ teaspoon butterscotch extract.
- Coffee Buttercream: Add 1 teaspoon coffee extract or 1 tablespoon (15 ml) Kahlúa.
- Amaretto Buttercream: Replace the milk with 3 tablespoons (45 ml) amaretto.
- Vanilla Bean Buttercream: Replace the vanilla extract with 1½ teaspoons vanilla bean paste or the contents of 1 vanilla bean.

Vanilla Bean Ice Cream

This ice cream is perfect on its own, but delicious alongside Bananas Foster à la Mode (page 157) and Caramel Amaretto Apricots with Toasted Almonds (page 158).

YIELD: 1½ PINTS (428 G)

⅔ CUP (160 ML) PLUS 2 TABLESPOONS (30 ML) SOY CREAMER, DIVIDED

1 CUP (235 ML) ALMOND MILK

½ CUP (100 G) SUGAR

½ VANILLA BEAN

4 TEASPOONS CORNSTARCH OR ARROWROOT

1 CAN (15 OUNCES OR 440 ML) COCONUT MILK

Combine ⅔ cup (160 ml) creamer, milk, sugar, and contents of vanilla bean in a medium saucepan over medium heat, whisking frequently to dissolve sugar. Bring to a boil, 5 to 7 minutes. In a small bowl, combine the 2 tablespoons (30 ml) creamer with cornstarch and stir to dissolve. Lower to a simmer and whisk in creamer and cornstarch.

Stir constantly until the mixture thickens, 5 minutes. Let cool. Stir in the can of coconut milk while still slightly warm, then let cool completely.

Freeze in an ice cream maker according to manufacturer's instructions.

Mascarpone

Inspired by the cheese, this cream is wonderful with fruit or incorporated into Italian desserts.

YIELD: 1½ CUPS (345 G)
---

8 OUNCES (227 G) VEGAN CREAM CHEESE

½ CUP (120ML) COCONUT CREAM

Whisk the cream cheese and coconut cream together. Refrigerate until ready to use.

RECIPE NOTE
You'll have about ½ cup (120 ml) leftover coconut cream from this recipe. Whip it up with some powdered sugar and top some cupcakes or dip fruit in it!

Acknowledgments

I would like to thank the following people:

My friends and family who agreed to taste test and offer honest feedback on every cupcake, doughnut, and cookie I made them eat several times a week!

Grandma, Mom, Dad, Kevin, Melissa, Alesha, Jessica, Jennifer, Aunt Debbie, Aunt Karen, and Uncle John.

The wonderful vegan ladies of Milwaukee—Jess, Lindsay, Colleen, Steph, and Lynn.

Thank you, Joni, for connecting me with Fair Winds Press, who made this book a reality. Thank you, Amanda Waddell and Heather Godin, for your kindness and for helping me through every step of the process.

My recipe testers from around the world, who volunteered their time, ideas, and baking supplies to make dozens of batches of dessert so these recipes would be tried and true! Thank you, Katja Haudenhuyse, Louzilla Ryan, Cindy Elder, Kelly Cavalier, Elizabeth Cook, Gina Garrett, Jorie Slodki, Amber Gilewski, Thalia C. Palmer, Amanda Rabe, Charis Powell, Tabitha Richelle, Debbie Prior, Olivia Allman, Erica Mendoza, Erin Goddard, Laura Ryan, Caitlin Johnson, Jessica Berglund, Jen Price, and Megan Hall.

All the amazing, compassionate people I've been fortunate to meet, online and in person, for being completely authentic, inspiring, and kind.

About the Author

Ever since discovering veganism as a teenager in 2005, Kelly Peloza has been baking, photographing, and writing about desserts. She is the author of *The Vegan Cookie Connoisseur* book and blog (www.thevegancookieconnoisseur.com) and often speaks about baking and vegan lifestyle at events around the United States.

A Chicagoland native, Kelly studied in Milwaukee to earn her B.F.A. in photography and writing. She loves reading, art, crafts, making project to-do lists, her dog Drake, and Gnocchi the bunny.

Index